T0375220

There Is No Escape, but That's a Good Thing

It's All Good

Dan Costello

authorHOUSE®

AuthorHouse™
1663 Liberty Drive
Bloomington, IN 47403
www.authorhouse.com
Phone: 1 (800) 839-8640

© 2016 Dan Costello. All rights reserved.

No part of this book may be reproduced, stored in a retrieval system, or transmitted by any means without the written permission of the author.

Published by AuthorHouse 10/12/2016

ISBN: 978-1-5246-4423-9 (sc)
ISBN: 978-1-5246-4421-5 (hc)
ISBN: 978-1-5246-4422-2 (e)

Library of Congress Control Number: 2016916791

Print information available on the last page.

Any people depicted in stock imagery provided by Thinkstock are models, and such images are being used for illustrative purposes only. Certain stock imagery © Thinkstock.

This book is printed on acid-free paper.

Because of the dynamic nature of the Internet, any web addresses or links contained in this book may have changed since publication and may no longer be valid. The views expressed in this work are solely those of the author and do not necessarily reflect the views of the publisher, and the publisher hereby disclaims any responsibility for them.

Contents

Once I chose the spirit,
I began to see a world in, which all was created equal.
And events, people, and things were opportunities
to experience love and render blessings. It was the
same world but now seen through new eyes.

Acknowledgments

My loving thanks to my wife, Karen, my four children, Danny, Patrick, Christian, and Jamie Marie for being my teachers. A special thanks to Reverend Corinne Ramage for being "The Teacher."

Surrender

> I've been driven many times to my knees by the overwhelming conviction that I have nowhere else to go.
>
> Abraham Lincoln

As morning came, I awoke with the same emptiness. It felt like an unwanted companion, a harsh teacher, or a drill sergeant. My fragile self cried out in desperation. I needed to do something. I moved my body in an attempt to relieve the pain and throw it off a bit so I could get a breath. I kneeled on the bed and looked out onto Main Street.

As I scanned the sunlit street, I saw a church. My eyes stopped on the hanging cross in the doorway. *A friend, a rescuer,* I thought. I still did not know what to do as the pain lingered in my throat and chest. I again looked at the cross with tears on my face. With an anguished gasp, I said, "I promise to dedicate my life to serve others—if you will rescue me from this hell."

I lay down and shut my eyes. I stayed in what felt like a burial position. I crossed my arms over my heart, and my feet were perfectly parallel. My mind began to recount the event that caused this suffering, and my eyes closed tighter. I tried to stop thinking. I felt immersed in a bath of white light—a warm, loving feeling passed through every cell in my body.

The spiritual veil was so thin that it changed me forever. I knew it was different, not normal, and not of this world. I felt loved, whole. I felt hugged in a warm embrace that lasted for eternity. The lone tear that made its way down my cheek felt cool.

I realized that my illumination was a state in, which enough barriers of forgetfulness had been deliberately dropped that a greater context suddenly presented itself. This experience allowed the inner light of my higher self to shine through as a profound lovingness.

When it was over, I didn't get any messages or visions. I jumped up and started doing push-ups. I put on Super Tramp's "In the Quietest

Moments," and got ready for class. My mind was soft with errant thoughts, but I had been given a divine charge.

I looked out on the same street, but it appeared brighter—illuminated by an internal light. I could only describe the residual feeling as a cushion of love.

As I ran past the smiling nun who was collecting money on Main Street for the poor, I stopped. Without hesitation, I gave her all my food money. She looked at me with a smile, and I ran on, waving my lacrosse stick with a spring in my step.

I ran right to the chapel and sat down. My heart was heavy, but it somehow felt light. The rest of this book begins and ends with my attempt to find this light again and extend it. I eventually realized that the light was broken up into spiritual technologies hidden in the chrysalis and vibrancy of my daily awakening. The following tools are truly vision-correction devices that help me see life in the light of peace and joy.

I researched other white light experiences and found them in the lives of two other powerful teachers: Bill Wilson of Alcoholics Anonymous and David Hawkins, MD, PhD. The lives they led after their spirit charges motivated me to build a better character and become a light in the world. The following tools have helped change my vision of self and the world. They worked in harmony with each other and began to synchronize with my intention to see through the lens of spirit. I used the following vision-correction tools daily as I bring inspiration and hope to the earth.

I am creating a life that reflects my own healing use of these tools and the wisdom I have gained from teaching them to countless others. The use of these tools and my dedication to healing suffering in me and others began to change my vision of life on earth. In time, my perception of life shifted from an unsafe world—in, which I was ill equipped to sustain peace and joy—to a timeless journey of unfolding potential held in complete love and forgiveness.

I am writing this book for three reasons: to elucidate the way for spiritual seekers who are using their life experiences as raw material for spiritual evolution, to give practical tools for anyone willing to have a better life, and to inspire those who are tired of the pain of suffering and dualistic lessons to pursue our divine right to see the world through spiritual vision.

Undoing truth would be impossible, but spiritual concepts—once learned, practiced, and integrated—will change one's vision. Once I realized what outdated concepts didn't fit my changing visions, I retrained my eyes and that began to change my concept of the outdated self. I was somehow still the same old me just wiser.

> *The greatest and most important problems in life are all in a certain way insoluble. They can never be solved only outgrown.*
>
> *Carl G Jung*
> *Circa 1930*

Instruction Manual

He who is not busy living is busy dying.

Bob Dylan

I OFFER the following spiritual technologies, which I have used formally since my awakening at twenty, to the reader as ways of vision transformation. I have used these tools for the past twenty-six years to bring out my best potential as a person. After much self-analysis, I found that the qualities that emerged were always available in my potential self behind that veil. I use these practices to find peace within myself and become a better person.

My intention was always to become a better healer for others, but my own healing is happening as well. I became aware of qualities in others and mimicked concepts and practices I believed would heal and correct my dysfunctional, shame-based vision of the world. We all teach who we are, but the character of some teachers stood out to me. I made it a point to study the holy and kind as I went along—even when I didn't feel worthy or capable of such behavior. I often acted "as if" until I integrated their models into daily practice in the form of the following tools. The use of these tools opened my spiritual heart.

This inner change was powerful enough, that my vision of myself and the external world was deeply affected. I began to see things through the light behind the veil of my higher self.

When I was a child, I wanted to help my parents find peace. This need for service came about powerfully due to my sensitive nature. I remember crying when I would hear the song "Eleanor Rigby" by the Beatles. I realized later that the help I wanted to give was the help I needed. Using these tools gave me a self-sufficient road map to become a better person and eventually an effective healer and teacher.

Once I realized that the work of transformation was unfolding my higher self, I became curious and excited to find and use a toolbox of tried-and-true mechanisms for change. The change could occur slowly or rapidly. Within a short time, everything I saw and all I did came from a spiritual intention. I began to see the world through spiritual vision. I was no longer fighting to gain fulfillment externally. I was seeing a world perfectly capable of meeting all my physical, emotional, and spiritual needs. All events, people, and things were suddenly gifts and opportunities to practice love. I began to realize I was no longer a victim of fear-filled inevitability, and I had a source of unlimited power at my disposal. I most effectively harnessed this power by using spiritual technologies. A technology when used in this books context is a body of knowledge or a spiritual, mental or physical practice that has the power to change aspects of the seekers life.

It became evident that being spiritual means seeing lessons and holiness in all things, people, and opportunities that come before and through us. The spiritual laws of abundance, attraction, and karma can be harnessed through the use of these tools to create the lives we dream of. By keeping our vows and commitments to self and others, we can have the energy to use these tools despite bouts of depression and fear of failure. The tools act as energizers and create a hopefulness that connects to our belief in their power.

I only had to choose the tool and allow its power to work without interference. They worked much like antibiotics. The right-minded concepts worked on my shame-based belief system. I began to see that I wasn't my self's broken, occluded vision of a victim. I was a unique expression of the divine energies that had always been present in my potential. I used tools like humility, honesty, devotion, patience, and compassion and became better at staying centered and making wiser decisions.

Please understand that each tool is healing and transformative in itself. The tools can be used in any order or manner we find most comfortable. We can adjust tools and their usage according to our life circumstances. With open eyes—through spiritual intention—can watch how opportunities arise to practice any tool we focus on.

Another beauty of having this supply of tools is that we can be creative with the tools we have already become familiar with. We can use many tools throughout the day (mentally and physically). From my experience, I knew the tools needed to be simple and easy to use, especially under pressure. I could focus on forgiveness as a contemplative idea and do higher self-filled service for a person in need at lunch. The tools can be utilized mentally or practiced literally in daily prayer, relationships, and crises. I also found that talking about the tools with others could reinforce their power in our own lives. I found that I was teaching what I needed to integrate more fully.

These tools hold a power to energize self-esteem. Each time we successfully practice these devices and notice their ever-present power to change the moment, we feel good about ourselves. As a result, we can choose to extend this to others. I have always tried to be kind, but once I had simple kindness as a constant companion, I felt safer socially and professionally. My body-mind is often at odds with the purpose of these tools, but through persistence, it relents (for the time being). When I don't use the tools and just act out of fear, I inevitably experience guilt and shame. I eventually used these two pain-filled helpers to learn. I would go back and study a new tool—or reinforce an existing one—to avoid this sharp and tender self-awakening system my body-mind set up to help me evolve.

I used some tools for a short period of time, and I used others daily. I would use a tool and realize it was harder to incorporate than another was at the time. I would look at why that was so. It became a productive search to uproot an existing fear in my belief system. I tried to forgive a person who had hurt me badly, and I wound up being able to use tolerance and kindness. I eventually got to forgiveness, but it was only after learning more from the tool of humility. Each tool sets the stage for the use of another. They assist each other like teammates on a sports team. The mere intention to use the spiritual mechanisms creates fertile ground for self integration and eventual transformation into higher consciousness, this higher vibration is still our unique being but will be referred to as both the holy and higher self.

The use of even one tool can be powerful enough to make a visible change in a person's character. My son is practicing gratitude exclusively at this point, and he is much more pleasant to deal with as a result. I don't mind helping Patrick more, especially praising his attitude of gratitude. These tools are also contagious and foster communion. Just saying thank you in the vicinity of other people increases the chances they will use gratitude in their practices.

We have a whole arsenal to negotiate what can be a very difficult endeavor: life on earth. The use of these tools helps develop positive character, and it can eventually affect your inner and outer life. I have found peace and joy more frequently as well as success at work and at home as a result of their usage. I am most impressed with my social transformation. I now say what I mean, and I rarely say it mean. I look forward to being around others, and I have recently begun to see more beauty in difficult people and situations. The best part of having this toolbox handy is the safety of reaching for a tried-and-true technology that I don't have to invent. I've felt and seen the power. The tools can empower us in all circumstances to grow as we become conduits of their healing power in the world.

I realized that I could gauge my success in how deeply integrated the tools were becoming by how frequently and automatically I reached for them. Success was rarely found in a feeling, but I used the tools wisely and with much success. I saw my changes first in the courage, perseverance and consistency in using the tools.

The tools are to be used by the unique individual who chooses to invoke them in any way needed. They are not mine; they are a gift from love itself. They are to be used creatively. This book is dedicated to awakening us to the power of *spiritual technology*. Spiritual technology describes thought tools that create readiness for learning and fuel willingness to let go of obstacles to growth. The devoted spiritual person journeys with a courageous heart in a dualistic land. To many, this earth school appears confusing and conflictual. If we look at the rules of living on earth, we clearly see into the core of dualistic learning. We see extremes everywhere, and we are constantly asked to make choices between them. All of these choices have an effect on our lives, and they serve as guidelines by which to learn.

My teacher once explained how spiritual truth is often hidden best in paradoxical wisdom. The title of this book is a good example of how something can be a prison house and a road to freedom. You will notice that one aspect of our thinking has no escape and always creates confusion, suffering, and death. This dead end combined with grace is enough to bring curiosity and deep desire to heal and strive for healing or in plain terms "peace of mind". The earth school with its specific laws can bring us up and out of this finite prison if we live with our eyes and ears open to the miracles available in the eternal now.

Duality by nature shows us where we are, and it gives us a map to where we would like to travel. The choices we make and their subsequent creations are our lives. I hope this book serves as a daily manual for spiritual seekers on any path to awaken. This guide helps us create the most vibrant lives available. The path of a modern-day seeker must be tailored to fit our lives and our levels of readiness for truth. Regardless of the technological interface we choose—ritual, religion, yoga, meditation, or any other form of technology designed to facilitate for us a more vibrant life—I hope something within these pages will be of loving service. To move in vibrant ways on the spiritual path takes a courageous heart. To move in vibrancy, we have to remember that the light and dark aspects of life and self must be embraced equally.

This evolution of mind and soul is best served once we become clear about what we are seeking. Are we seeking consciousness on a higher plane? Are we seeking peace of mind or health of body? These questions help readers negotiate the following thought tools and identify the ones that fit best. One must journey with an open heart into the belly of the beast. This is called *dualistic learning*. Establishing clear goals, at least periodically, throughout the journey will help reassure us that the trip into the higher self is worth it.

To begin any journey, especially one of the heart and mind, we must delve deeply into what could be new ground and desire holiness above all else. In this case, *holiness* does not necessarily refer to religious correctness or interfere with any community goal. Instead, *holiness* as stated earlier refers to a state of being that I will refer to here after as either the holy or *the higher self*. This self is the dualistic counterpart of the body's identity self, which is an accumulation of many experiences and attachments that are a combination of our karmic propensities and earth-life programming. The self identifies with a separate body in space and time and is run by a level of consciousness designed and often motivated by lack, fear, and victimhood learned in the past.

The holy or higher self—our actualized, most integrated self—is so natural to being that it brings love, wisdom, and invulnerability in any and all circumstances. The higher self is a spiritual entity that is not limited to intellect and the dualistic human heart. For many, the power of this soul expression will take on a unique form in our lives and it will express itself no matter what our spiritual goals are. This will happen as we allow ourselves to be continually taught by everything on the divine path and move through our fears and naiveties.

Spiritual fulfillment is a very reachable goal if we remain steadfast in using the thought changes that allow the higher self to appear. To evolve spiritually, we must enlist many tools that are more powerful than intellect and prior learning. The thought tools in this manual are designed to sow seeds in the body-mind through the intellect, and with the help of the neutral witness mind-set, our learning can eventually burst the limited way we see things and allow the higher mind to emerge. The higher mind is analogous with our right-mind.

The higher mind is the all-knowing decision maker of the higher self, and is connected to a knowingness the body mind lacks. And if we listen openly, its divine guidance helps us realize that every step taken brings us one step closer to spiritual fulfillment, whether it appears to take the traveler forward or backward. It might also become clearer from this healing thought that everything on the spiritual journey was divinely placed and inspired. Imagine that all occurrences—whether we label them without dualistic words like good or bad or holy or evil—were somehow perfect for our healing and subsequent soul evolution on earth.

Spiritual fulfillment has an opportunity to be felt once we surrender to life with our eyes and hearts open, knowing that the highest good is always being served with every step. Surrendering is an imperative tool on a path that often feels unfamiliar.

The use of this manual and familiarization with the tools and concepts being taught will create a fertile ground for walking this journey. The fertile ground that one who is seeking any goal on the spiritual path is one of constant consciousness. Where you place your consciousness is where you awaken. What you look at has life. If you do not see it, it does not exist for you. It only exists outside of your perception. This is a time to do our best to know everything.

If you are walking on rough terrain, it will be important to know and be aware of its presence. Fertile ground is everywhere, and with our eyes and hearts open in surrender; we will see all the lessons with better clarity. This revelation combined with our dedicated use of the tools prescribed within this manual can act as the fuel for evolution on earth. Every situation properly perceived becomes an opportunity to heal. The strength of our commitments and our willingness to surrender what we wish to see will truly plant peace, love, and wisdom in our lives so we can serve our fellow humans and live in oneness as a holy self on earth.

Please keep in mind the following questions as you proceed:

- What are your spiritual goals?
- How far have you gotten in reaching your spiritual goals?
- What is working—and what is not working?
- Are you stuck in any way?
- What are your obstacles?
- How willing are you to see through new eyes?
- How confident or certain are you of your success in evolving into your holy self?

We must accept finite disappointment but never lose infinite hope

Martin Luther King
Circa 1960's

Neutral Witness

We are all serving a life sentence in the dungeon of self

Cyril Connolly

A SPIRITUAL seeker who is willing to incorporate spiritual tools every day to increase conscious awareness may pique the curiosity for additional ways to ignite the spirit and empower the search for spiritual fulfillment. This spiritual intention is a high calling that naturally moves people in vibrant ways.

Living a vibrant life is a combination of extremes; it is a blending of conflicting earth lessons and movements of the soul in our daily lives. Navigating these power-filled lessons and movements calls for tools and technologies that give strength and clarity. Soul lessons often go unnoticed, but they appear in light and dark occurrences. For instance, they could be about forgiveness or compassion, but they all lead to revelations that help connect us to healing. To help understand one of the more powerful tools, we can use the simple analogy of an empty room. Picture yourself sitting in a comfy chair between two open windows, and then allow any thoughts, beliefs, or inspirations coming through the window and going out the other. We should become better at observing as many as possible from the comfy chair and make choices about which ones to hold for self-guidance or additional information. Curiosity is eventually replaced by staying conscious, surrendering to any obstacles that block our progress, and staying the course. Curiosity can create willingness to go into our shadow self which has an empowering effect on all we do on the path to awakening.

The neutral witness tool is a tremendously powerful state that can be considered a foundation of spiritual evolution technology. This tool goes by many names and is reached for in many practices and on many paths. Some call it the "observer" or the "inventory taker," and it is behind the use of meditation in many cultures. It is generally agreed upon that intended focus is imperative for progressing consciously as people or as spiritual seekers. The willingness to access a neutral space and observe what goes on in the body-mind (and acts as a door for divine wisdom) is imperative if we are to sort through beliefs and limiting or self-destructive thought streams.

The spiritually minded seek to transcend the body or intelectual mind altogether. This acts as a two-way lens that can be envisioned as a place between the body-mind and higher mind. Reinforcing the curiosity created from learning or suffering gives us a place to observe, discern, and allow. This distance can create more opportunities to choose positive practices—like tolerance, acceptance, and forgiveness—as we navigate the divinely inspired lives we walk.

The neutral witness helps us observe and bypass past programming and agendas to see messages in the dark and light. This is extremely helpful as we look for truth and love since they hide in our limited perceptions. The conscious use of light and dark gives us the ability to understand lessons as we walk through our days. The contrasts they create actually give maximum clarity despite our emotions. The neutral witness is a higher mind tool that exists out of time. It can observe past and present, and it is so wondrous.

When we become sharply awakened to lessons learned through physical pain or pleasure or emotional comfort or discomfort, these clues still have to be processed and integrated into daily life through thought to help with transformation. It is harder when we try to decipher lessons from the emotional part of our lives because of the diversity and distance from what could be more easily ascertained from thinking or higher mind. When we look at it without all the emotional energy of longing for the past or misperceptions about the past, clarity comes more easily. As we will see later, it doesn't always serve us to just have light lessons, given the nature of perception to cover up pain and suffering and minimize its blessings.

This tool of neutrality actually serves as a gate to a beyond that brings the inner voice into alignment with wisdom. A meaningful use of higher self-evolving wisdom is the effort that helps us to focus on changing beliefs that block the awareness of our innate divinity. We can proceed with confidence if we use spiritual technology to go about awakening with more peace. The daily use of the neutral mind space increases the willingness and faith in the use of this mighty tool. Human choices also yield better results, and our levels of spiritual vision grow. Spiritual vision is a way of seeing only meaning in all that comes before us in our daily lives.

Observing any dysfunction or misalignment in neutrality accelerates movement away from dysfunction and deepens healing. When we move to neutrality to get clarity, we are more in the flow of divine time. That allows for a combination of more faith, patience and wisdom as we proceed. We make better choices. In general, neutrality helps us grow a seamless relationship to all experiences, and it brings to light the divine underbelly of what lies within.

As dedicated spiritual seekers, we are constantly being asked to observe without the judgment of good and bad and move beyond to an initial lens of either fear or love. Through the use of humility and spiritual contemplation, one can feel and see the positive fruits and mistakes of past choices and use these understandings to rely on a wisdom that is increasingly accessed through the use of the neutral witness. This observation system also allows us to use the body-mind to set and reach finite goals until they are no longer needed to journey.

One of the bigger obstacles the spiritual seeker can encounter is the lack of ability and confidence in being able to discern the impulsive thinking of body-mind and the divine voice of higher self. The subtle whisper of higher self easily gets overpowered by the shouting and impatient voice of self. With the neutral witness in place, one can see and hear better. This allows for patience and the oneness alluded to in many spiritual and scriptural writings. In this oneness, listening comes without effort.

In the sacred space of neutrality, we can allow things to pass us by that could derail or detour peace. This marriage of body-mind and divine mind becomes one and works more practically in our daily lives. We watch in a way "from above the battle field". The neutral witness allows us to take constant inventory of our belief structures as they evolve, shed, or update positions that no longer apply. There are higher and more inclusive compassionate truths.

The truth on earth for dedicated spiritual seekers is variable and constantly evolves. We must stay open to guidance and remain awake in humble learning. The truths we believed and needed to hold at different stages on the path of evolution no longer are appropriate and resonate as love.

The world of dualistic learning allows for extreme experiences and extreme teachers. As discussed earlier, pain is as powerful a teacher as love, but they do not feel the same. Every choice on earth seems to have a consequence (good or bad), given our limited ability to understand the divine mind. We can often default to feeling victimized by something or someone. Choices that are made impulsively and without discernment can make our lives seem confusing and fearful.

In a state of neutrality, we can use witnesses to play any tape. We can rewind old tapes for lessons, watch old lessons again, or fast-forward to future choices to avoid certain consequences. We would be better off remembering that all lessons are expressions of the sacred journey. They are being brought to attention only to be healed and teach—not to victimize (as the body-mind would have us believe.

When we feel overwhelmed, we can be pulled in by impulsively acting in ways that are not sorted out through neutrality. When we rely on perception and impulse together, we run the risk of creating choices that have consequences that have to be undone for resolution.

Mistakes are a big part of the learning process on earth. No matter how hard we try to be perfect, there is no way out of this inevitable trial and error since we have limited minds. The tools described in this book allow for learning that builds higher self-love and compassion as we navigate this confusing school.

All choices and temptations are opportunities for learning. We are never doing anything wrong. Some choices may be less fruitful, and the series of events or outcomes set forth by these less fruitful choices may require some undoing. The more destructive choices might have more to undo, but the soul is eternally innocent. Our spiritual laws on earth although apparently relevant scientifically are also based on the physical laws. For example, cause and effect can be called karma in another sense we are all bound by both physical and spiritual laws. Be certain that they all Influence the mental, emotional, and spiritual aspects of the search for holy self.

The soul serves as a spiritual bank account. It stores our learning and helps create lessons that are especially designed for awakening. If we do not heal a lingering resentment toward another, it can hold the body-mind hostage. This impulsively creates suffering through the attraction of what is perceived as a dark teacher with painful lessons.

This pain-induced learning builds pressure and can create confusion and hopelessness, which can cause us to use outdated coping strategies.

Even though going backward can be uncomfortable, it is part of the dualistic learning experience. It helps in the creation of courageous hearts. Neutrality offers us distance from what is going on in our lives. It sheds light on the lessons that hide in the dark. It helps us unwrap the lessons, navigate around dark teachers, and avoid suffering. We can intend to learn only by light lessons of love and intellectual learning, but it might not serve us best.

When we incorporate surrender, we allow the present teacher to do its best work. The neutral witness is also a state of sacred heart that fully and completely accepts all that occurs in our lives as being divinely inspired by Love while retaining an individual mind-set based on personal experience. As we become more familiar with the divine mind and its whisper of higher vibrational truths, we might be able to hold gratitude for the dark lessons and teachers and practice levels of forgiveness that change our perspectives.

Once one becomes more certain on the path of surrender and more familiar in the previously unfamiliar lane of neutrality, one can choose to enter them quickly and frequently. As in other spiritual endeavors, a curious stirring gives way to certain movements into mastery. In the beginning of a relationship with neutrality, one might be able to access a still place that feels appealing. The part of neutrality that is a still point can be a place of peace while one observes the battlefield of dualistic learning from above. The still point can also serve as a reminder to return often.

In summary, the neutral witness perspective is a technology that one can access best through the practice of surrender. Once we become more familiar and versed at the nonjudgmental tolerance found in this divine tool, we can develop clarity and confidence of vision that help us observe and bypass obstacles to our awakening. This practice can also serve to create the best possible life on earth. This ability to be fully present on the earth and access the divine mind and all it brings with it is our inheritance. Grace, peace, joy, and invulnerability are our rewards for the persistence and courage it takes to live as spiritual beings in such a challenging realm.

Through the practices of meditation and contemplation, we see the mind as a vessel with many rooms. The ultimate goal is to access this room as a tool when it is needed most—in the middle of our lessons, in the heat of the day, and in the grace of walking the sacred journey on earth.

Oneness and the holy self are accessible on the other end of the threshold of the door that is held open by the heart of the neutral witness state of higher mind.

We must learn to see the world anew.

—Albert Einstein
Circa 1930

Sacred Journey

Awareness is therapy per se.

Fritz Perls

SPIRITUAL FULFILLMENT is attained in the surrender to live with eyes and hearts open, knowing that the highest good is served with each step taken. No matter how far you look back or project forward, life is holy in the church of the holy mind. Our life occurrences are often shrouded by drama, but they are the raw material for awakening. If we journey with faith and a belief that we are loved unconditionally by the divine rather than wandering in fear of impending punishment, we can better tolerate feelings of inevitability and overcome the limited beliefs the mind uses in order to keep the body safe. This will help us strive more fearlessly toward any spiritual goal we have chosen. For most, these goals are unconscious. They are accessible with effort. Imagine that our every step, in a backward or forward direction, is blessed and inspired. We must continually trust— even when our lives are spiraling out of control or meeting our needs in ways only hoped for—that both directions are one in holiness.

To understand this better, we must remember that the ability to see clearly what is of divine origin is occluded in most of our lives. We see with a pair of eyes that is so limited by its need to reference the past and project its own agenda that we barely have a clue when truth is speaking in the eternal. We attempt to discover who we are in what we think we should be or in what others think we should be. We move in a world of shadows, going back and forth between grace and obscurity. The good news is that these extremes of light and darkness trigger experiences that energize us to grow and evolve in ways we might not have consciously planned.

The human mind is always looking for experiences and relationships to define itself through contrast. The compare-and-contrast approach normally used by the body-mind helps us feel rewarded, remembered, and recognized, and it is exactly what is needed on this level as we strive for self-definition. The self can be seen and understood with greater clarity in the light of someone or something else—an accomplishment or failure of a goal.

It takes many vantage points (persons, objects, experiences) to know who it is as an individual. That's why relationships, whether dark or light, are sacred. When looked at through the tool of gratitude, they are tremendously powerful. Perception acts as a constantly changing mirror of body self with its made up character traits. When we glimpse and grasp to feel an anchor, we come away with a transient story of a persona that grows, shrinks, and invariably changes. Who we are perpetually ebbs and flows. We live at the mercy of the shifting sands of physical reality and the conditionally based relationships that make up our lives. The self acts like a stunt double for soul experiences as we strive to keep our soul promises and search for fulfillment in this finite physical school called earth.

The search for self-fulfillment is perfect. Its limited experiences bring vibrancy and curiosity for something beyond. In a journey that is deeply devoted to uncovering the higher self, we will eventually be challenged to discard the accumulated, patchwork self. The willingness and vibrant movement through mistakes and victories can provide the heightened compassion and courage needed for uncovering the higher self. Infinite abilities unfold as more and more aspects of the holy self emerge from their patient hiding places, seeking resolution and harmony for the conflicting nature of the self. This self we identify with a body has a story that we might not like. What if our endeavors in an experiential world of change and resistance are leading us to the realization that nothing in the world is ours or worth keeping?

At this point of fertile awareness, we can choose to delve deeper into the sacred journey, spurred on by the stirrings of curiosity. It can be frightening to travel where you have never been and do so with trust. To remedy this, we must loosen our expectations for how the journey should look and relinquish all judgment.

The body-mind habitually evaluates spiritual experience through an outdated self-evaluation system called "the past" as it tries to judge new experiences. When using this outdated and inappropriate comparison system, we must be mindful of self-forgiveness in an effort to quell the bubbling up of fear that is stored in a body of pain living in the *preconscious* or unconscious.

Since we are always at the mercy of the law of duality, we often go back to old self-coping styles like manipulation, denial, bullying, ritual, and other rigid patterns from the past. This can become a gift so we can heal on the deepest levels. These skills are primitive and only serve to reinforce fear and lack unless we allow there integration into a "new holy self" emerging out of the balance of our dark and light aspects. As we evolve, we occasionally regress and use them again in certain situations.

Until we have progressed enough spiritually to only react from more of a higher self-energy field, old coping skills are a necessity so as not to leave us defenseless in a challenge or temptation. They also serve in duality to help clarify effectiveness. Without the knowledge that we can return to the familiar, we might abandon the spiritual journey or compromise its meaningfulness, leaving us misaligned and without the wisdom we crave.

What are our spiritual goals? This question should be constantly revisited. Spiritual seekers will be constantly asked to choose to become the purest, most authentic expression of love possible, but all will choose what is needed for fulfillment in the present.

The sacredness in all journeys—no matter how light or dark—is seen as we acquire fulfillment on some level. This sacredness is seen in our devotion and can take us on countless paths—even ones we label evil or mediocre. Every soul expression is divinely held and supported and can help our integration and transformation if we keep our eyes open to the divinity within each opportunity. Spiritual devotees in the past usually reach for "heaven" in any way they deem meaningful. This book proposes that mistakes are perfect in their ability to teach and awaken. True nature is an impenetrable heavenly innocence. A forgiveness mind will remove the preprogrammed obstacles of judgment and attack to acquire the knowledge to live vibrantly. To handle this corrupted belief in sin, we must confess transgressions or regressions and move to more fertile ground for the evolution of consciousness.

Mistakes aren't mistakes; they are just products of limited sight. If we accept that concept, we can move past forgiveness and go about undoing what was poorly chosen. The practice of self-forgiveness and acceptance enables us to feel the power of the lesson. In hindsight, we often realize it was the best we could have done at that place in time. As we change our beliefs and surrender, the journey unfolds. We are not always going to understand this right of way and might come as a future revelation after more learning or traumatic experiences have taken place.

Since we're used to our minds being full of fear, we await our punishments. My hope is that the concepts being espoused in this book are analogous to building a ladder. Each technology serves as a rung to allow for a higher consciousness to empower choices. These choices increase joy and make us carriers of the technology to others.

In this new sacred model, there is no punishment because there's never a victim. Only love shows us the way to our lessons. Each choice attracts these lessons, and through cause and effect, we have a chance to learn. This type of journey into the heart of light and dark might bring us deeper into conflict, but with the help of the laws of dualistic challenges and cause and effect, we can grow and gain revelations as we integrate and transform. Each time we use a tool from the spiritual toolbox, we put a rung on the ladder of consciousness. As we climb higher, we move more firmly into the sacred heart of grace—and toward fulfillment.

Two of the results of seeing life as a sacred journey into the unfolding of the higher self are the growing and holy-self-generated feelings of certainty and overall love. Through this set of spiritual eyes, one doesn't see fault or sin. It sees mistakes. Mistakes can be forgiven, and in this model of evolution, all are innocent and ignorant. Through a forgiveness mind, we can undo problems in the future. Without the need to repress the pain of guilt and shame, we clearly see our divine lesson presented in a welcoming light.

This growing familiarity with innocence allows us to stop evaluating spiritual gains and losses. We can realize how limited and faulty our self-judgment systems really are when we see them from neutral standpoints. What if perceived gains were really consolatory regressions? What if loss was really breaking meaningless habits? How can we evaluate the gains and losses?

I chalked off many clients as unmovable in resistance or lacking in effort until they became heroes in recovery. When we end up surrendering to trust and letting go of controlling outcomes, an influx of grace can shine through for the greater good. When we use neutrality and step back from the need to control, we have better chances of getting what we need.

There is no wrong way to interpret life's happenstance. Some ways are enriching, and other ways are less so. As we become more conscious and fertile through conscious practices, we start seeing that life is a perfect school. It is not a battleground or a torture chamber of longing. Lessons can appear in nearly everything that happens. Other people can be seen as sacred teachers who are designed to be mirrors and illuminators.

In teachings and seminars, people ask, "What if I miss my lesson?" I can tell you from experience that they will come around again in perfect timing. With faith in the process, we can sometimes see that we were not ready at that earlier junction. The practice of neutrality and surrender help us use all occurrences to grow. Even temptation can help us grow since it strokes the mind and keeps us seeking fulfillment through finiteness. This type of seeking always has a shelf life, which can be a great blessing.

Take, for instance, the journey of addiction. I know many people who became convinced that short-term fixes were "no escape." The journey on earth appears complicated and obscure, but it can serve as a perfect guide to a place most have only dreamed of. We must journey with courageous hearts and the willingness to surrender what we think it must be for and how it should be.

Still the searcher must ride the dark horse, racing alone in his freight.

Neil Young

Duality

He who comprehends the darkness in himself, to him the light is near.

Carl G Jung
The Red Book

IF THE goal of spiritual evolution is to let go of the meaningless, we must learn what is meaningful. Duality is the perfect mechanism to teach us what we are not and what we really are as divine beings. In the journey to peace, we are given the gift of free will to release the choice for conflict and allow peace's presence. When we choose anything other than peace, we are choosing conflict.

In looking at the importance of understanding duality and its value to spiritual evolution, we must first embrace the fact that the human mind can only know something by contrast, comparison, or remembrance. These finite tools call for a mechanism that facilitates clarity; once we are clear on something, we can move beyond, allow, and ultimately let go of what's not valuable.

Duality is the divine mechanism of clarity in a land that has many hidden teachings and obscure lessons. One must constantly consider the possibility that, by using right-minded vision, there is no good or bad. There is only the meaningful or its absence. The limitation of self makes the curiosity and desire that channels the energy needed to strive for spiritual evolution. When we tire of meaningless striving for fulfillment, we realize that suffering and conflict no longer serve us. We may develop a desire for a *beyond state*. This state pulls us into higher levels of consciousness, bringing a better quality of life.

A major theme in a dualistic learning environment is the fruitless repeating of mistakes. This can clearly define the valueless illusions we live by. Once we become tired of repeating meaningless and fruitless behaviors and using old tools like self-reproach and blame, we can begin to integrate new behaviors that render better outcomes. These light-infused technologies, with their grace-filled results, are in direct contrast to the lessons of dark teachers and their suffering and need for undoing and forgiveness.

As we progress along the path, we can choose tools like humility and meekness. The repetition of old lessons can still be a source of strength, fostering the willingness to deeply surrender. If healing is to occur, attention must be paid to. These lessons without judgement. Humility and the understanding of them can teach us the best route to any goal.

Practices like contemplation can enhance duality. Guidance and counseling bring insight with the repeated use of the neutral witness. Ultimately, the familiarization and acceptance of duality as a benevolent teacher and helper minimizes the mind's tendency to see through the *victim default lens*. Without understanding that life works for us through rules like duality, we might become confused and believe that life works against us. Faith that has no doubt is dead faith.

A challenge often encountered by spiritual seekers arises once they become used to seeing lessons in mundane mistakes, interactions, and casual relationships. The minds block helpful information with a haze of denial and ignorance. Newness is in definite contrast to the past. It is easy to accept white lies, poor discipline, or slight resentments without keeping mindful vigilance.

The ability to recognize and accept the teachings in duality gives us the best chance to balance human nature. This equilibrium is the doorway out of the constant push and pull found in resistance and defense that keeps our body-mind and human nature in place as the definer of our lives. This can lead us back to the incorporation of true neutrality as a major tool in evolution.

In true neutrality, finiteness and infiniteness are equally important experiences, but they are not equal. Finiteness is about time, process, measurable growth, separation, boundaries, goals, achievements, and completion. All those things have endings. Infiniteness is about soul awakening, resonance, unity, expansiveness, and oneness, which live in the eternal realm. The beauty of finite existence is seen in its ability to call forth the desire to expand and balance. To complete any growth-filled project or heal any miscreation, we need to balance finiteness by observing its consequence in any way accessible at the time and learn its infinite truth. All possibilities are already present in duality to be explored, and correction and truth are integrated until transformation can occur.

The belief that light and dark are polar opposites must be let go if we are to move beyond. They are, and they are not. Once we come to understand that there is no escape from the rules of duality and stop perceiving the movement of light and dark as journeys in opposite directions, we can balance all experiences. This balance offers the constant option to view all interaction "from above the battlefield." To clearly be open to what is in front of us to learn is greatly enhanced by our acceptance of dark lessons.

For most of us, lessons of love are easily accepted, but to a mind whose job it is to avoid pain, it is difficult to stand tall in darkness and still be a happy learner. A spiritual seeker is often asked to reframe his or her view of life from the perspective of higher self and practice seeing the hidden teaching in all occurrences. Balance is so powerful when used to handle dualistic lessons, and it takes much vigilance to not choose one extreme over another. To hide in the darkest dark or brightest light is tremendously limiting in the ability to teach. Even though it seems more appealing to stay in light and deny dark lessons in life and self, devoted seekers constantly move into unfamiliar territory with courage.

The more balanced we become in neutrality; the more wisdom can be accessed from the mind. The belief that the journey of good or light is more desirable because of outcomes stems from the human need for measurement and self-evaluation. The spiritual journey on earth, once it is understood through balance and duality, is not resisted. It leads to the same destination without the need to value the self as other than a helper in the process of communication and evolution on earth. The destination looks and feels different for everyone, but ultimately, it is called evolution and fulfillment. In the end, balance and duality lead to a beyond where there is no more trial, grace, conflict, or love. There is only a glorious blending of it all.

How do we travel in two directions simultaneously? We can answer this question when we become versed in predominantly seeing from the neutral witness lens. This place is not a gray area or a dilution of light and dark. To see it, we must imagine a gray that is a combination and vibrancy of the brightest light and deepest dark—and we can come close. I am only getting glimpses of this place, and it feels new and refreshing.

In conclusion of this all-important chapter about spiritual evolution through duality, we must realize that if we keep on this trajectory, we are destined to serve as integrated versions of what is here now. We are in complete harmony with all that is, and we are in total acceptance.

Duality is the ultimate reference guide and measurement tool. In this model, love is defined by no love. It sometimes feels like hate, sadness, or unhappiness. In the quest to spiritually evolve on earth, there is nothing to conquer. There is no enemy. Love is defined by hate and no love. Happiness is defined by sadness, and the self brings on the self. As we move toward becoming more familiar with constantly seeing through neutrality, we no longer need extreme opposites to understand who we are and which way to go. We will rarely find ourselves seeking the opposite side of the coin. In true neutrality, opposites come to meet each other. When the yes and no are one, the road is easily traveled into the heart of the holy self and others.

The goal on earth varies, but when we use our experiences to measure our intentions and let go of the outcomes, the journey stays fresh. Through faith—even faith that carries doubt—the quality of our lives can be enhanced. Clarity always allows better choices. Choices are the fuel for all movement (regressive and revelatory). Because of the healing power of duality and the fact that there is no escape from its laws, we can be saved from ignorance.

Surrender

We cannot change anything unless we accept it.

Helen Keller
Memoirs

EVERY MORNING is an important portal for a spiritual seeker. This first awakening is when self-discipline can begin to search for the neutral vantage point that allows for the clear observation of the mind-set we are in at that time. When we anchor in the safe house of our witness, we can discern between fearful mind and loving mind. We begin to align and center on divine/loving mind for our day and walk about more consciously. This initial practice helps us regain the power to make the most enlightened choices. The loving mind always provides unrivaled, pure inspiration. This mind is new, and it is not tethered to past programming or the agenda of the body-mind. The loving mind moves in the divine flow of grace in the now.

Each morning, if we intend to feel balanced and fulfilled before stepping out into a world, we must be awake in our lessons. Many seekers attempt to live unconditionally and forgive as they navigate their daily lives. Once we realize that we cannot always get what we need from the world or normal perceptions, curiosity and courage can move us forward into relationships with the mind (where divine helpers and wisdom beyond our normal thinking are available to assist). This can be accessed through things like prayer, service, or the sacred practice of surrendering. This sacred time in the morning is an optimum time to become conscious, bring the mind under control, and access wisdom.

The body-mind speaks first as it gets its feet planted on a ground that could shift and gives impulsive counsel as it lives its fear-based agenda. Much of this fear is fueled by a reservoir of stored guilt and resentment whether conscious or unconscious to get us to react. The ultimate goal of many seekers is becoming a conduit of divinity on earth.

As a holy being/self is awakened by using the technologies described in this book and other spiritual texts and pathways, we move closer to spiritual and personal potentialities. As we gain more confidence in tools like surrendering, our relationships with the self become clearer through synchronicities and grace. All we are and ever will be can be accessed through the acquisition and living of the higher self. The holy self brings all its power from its divine source—not the outside world or our perception skills. It eventually becomes evident that answers are contained within our daily lives, but we need triggers to activate that wisdom.

This aspect of innocent and natural being brings confidence to a daunting journey into new spiritual territory. When we surrender trust in the belief of the higher self, we can access a higher consciousness, which has knowledge our mind has yet to learn. To surrender, we must drop the existing tools, beliefs, and defenses we use to navigate in a world we only see in obscurity. In doing so, it becomes evident that the mind is the direct denial of mind—and the two can never meet.

The tool of surrender gives us a place for our problems. When coupled with patience, which is a source of comfort, we can live as spiritual beings in the human experience. We are the children of our own choices and lives. If we use tools like surrender, we will eventually realize that innate divinity is our natural state. The ability to tolerate diversity in the world will have more meaning as we become familiar with the art of surrendering. We can learn to surrender, trust what goes on in the mind, and hold only what is accessed from the higher mind.

Surrender becomes a very important tool once we realize that resisting or fighting to overcome human nature only creates a circuitous route that reinforces its hold. Denying any part of who we are leaves us incomplete. The level of mind we live in normally is not interested in leaving, and it appears to be a space of thought we create to keep us busy in our apparent ignorance.

If everything is part of a divine plan to evolve, all aspects of the self can be raw materials for growth. This apparent state of ignorance has led to many practices, rituals, and beliefs in an attempt to hold onto the elusive safety net (but only creates conflict and confusion). These learned and limited beliefs and practices serve perfectly in a dualistic learning environment to teach us what works and what doesn't.

We continue to put much of our efforts into doing things in the outside world as opposed to focusing on getting to know our minds and access our spirits. Surrender is a tool of *undoing* and only requires the letting go of what we once thought we couldn't live without.

When one surrenders, one becomes willing to allow others or other beliefs to be in control. We can actually surrender in stages or surrender thoughts, practices, and behaviors. This multifaceted tool is so versatile that it can be used in any and all challenges. The endeavor of using past programming and its limitations can actually increase the development of a steadfast willingness and devotion to spiritually evolve, but it will always lead to the same frustrating impasse due to its poor ability to move us forward. No matter what the fuel for the striving for fulfillment—fear, lack, or love—we might still need anchors and weapons to return to for safety. This can be beneficial when it reinforces old coping skills of fruitlessness.

Once we become familiar with surrendering and incorporating it into our toolboxes for spiritual evolution, we will find a warm embrace. Spiritual seekers are often faced with emotional soul expressions that leave them feeling vulnerable and clinging to what might feel like outdated and limited human tools. Rituals, petitions, prayers, manipulation, aggressiveness, and thoughts of victimhood or attack reinforce a self in which there is no escape.

To surrender is to trust and allow faith to be the guide. Previously, we trusted in things others taught—and they were reinforced through constant usage. These mind tools and thought structures gave us technology that served as stepping-stones, which can be seen and measured. This past learning can hide the holy self and obscure any appreciation and awareness of our own divine heritage and spiritual worthiness. This becomes evident when we look at the types of relationships created when we believe we can be punished or separated from our own source. It's like a sunbeam being separated from the sun—it just fails to be.

One of the immediate benefits of using surrender is that we are less compelled by fear-based motivation and more drawn to change once self-love moves into place. It is imperative to constantly remind ourselves that the holy self is the divine in us and the essence of soul. It is not at the mercy of anything in the world of form and change. This is reinforced because of surrender's inherent ability to invoke feelings like resolution and peace, which are fleeting in the world. It takes great diligence and courage to surrender daily issues—whether they are extreme or mundane.

Once we feel this love and have more certainty in our divine heritage, we begin to rely less on fear-based tools. We feel less separation from the divine source. Surrendering also teaches us new levels of trust as we are guided. Surrender is the energy that drives faith because it requires focusing on who and what we trust, and it requires letting go of outcomes. This leap of faith through the door of trust takes a courageous heart: filled with a vibration of orange for (self-strength) and red (power) as seen through an electron microscope.

Once we begin to allow ourselves to surrender, things we might have been using as resistances to hearing divine guidance can drop away. Journeying without direction will increase awareness of higher self-certainty. It is difficult but imperative to realize that even self-destructive behavior can be divinely inspired. Some of these apparent blocks take the form of resentments, low self-esteem, and the belief in lack or victimhood of any kind. We might begin to acquire sacred hope and promise within the unfamiliar and initially vulnerable terrain of misdirection.

Once we develop a familiar relationship with the divine, we can see the beauty of what comes out of the heart of grace. One of these gifts is a divine promise. This promise is analogous to a bank account that already has all the money promised, cashed, and available for usage.

Surrender especially comes in handy during introspection as we bravely accept and dislodge the darkness. Once we surrender with humility and stay anchored in the neutral witness state of mind, our inefficient beliefs, programmed resentments, and self-attack experiences come to the surface and heal. To help with this vital evolutionary practice, imagine surrendering and standing naked—disrobed of our costumes, excuses, and defenses.

It is natural for the mind to perceive nakedness as vulnerability. Once we begin to experience the sacred holy self and feel its certainty, being that vulnerable would be so intolerable and rarely attempted if we are not standing in the brilliance of the light or clothed in the self. This light comes from the relenting belief in our innate divinity and the unconditional support available through love. The sacred love that is inherent in the willingness to believe in our innate holiness gives us the courage to surrender all that tempts us into giving up on our goals. Sometimes we have to "fake it to make it."

We can dare to believe that enlightenment in all its variations is our inheritance as children of the divine. The revelation that is apparent once we surrender the journey itself is that our awakening was always by the grace of the divine—and was not something earned.

The deeper we surrender along the journey to peace and the more circumstances we use it in this place of mental peace with increased faith, the better it works. It is like living at the edge of a cliff of unknowing and jumping off without concern for the landing. We feel deep security in the certainty and inevitability that the landing will be perfect. We might not always get what we want or feel it in expected ways, but we will always get what we need in order to flourish. The mind, with its fear-based survival skills, wants to constantly control the whole journey. Therefore, it is through our efforts to bypass these thoughts and continued vigilance that our use of any spiritual tool succeeds.

As we grow accustomed to using spiritual tools, it is normal—and appropriate—to rely on old tools. It is tremendously helpful to be patient with the integration of truth and the technologies for living spiritually on earth. If we need to regress, we must leave a trail of breadcrumbs. Regression is a teaching tool and is not be used as an excuse to beat oneself up. We have poor understanding at times about what's best for the soul's evolution. Something that looks like a regression might be a result of a major step forward and needed for safety in the newness occurring. This supposed step backward or mistake could be just the thing that gives clarity to a wiser choice in the future.

The evolutionary journey is always showing us where to go and where love exists in its dualistic fashion, but we can barely see it. Certain attitudes, practices, and experiences can increase our confidence and courage as we progress. Living consciously as we utilize open listening and spiritual vision will help us see the divine in all of what the eternal now brings. Awakening is a process when a shift from perception to spiritual vision occurs. New paths open for us. While nothing external has changed, everything is different.

Imagine surrendering all experiences and people in our lives. When we learn to travel with trust and use surrendering as a way to be guided by a higher mind that can see the whole picture, we develop confidence in being divinely inspired. We are able to see divine signs in all things— even tragedies and challenges that were previously judged to be dark.

Surrendering could mean allowing occasional periods of regression into old behavior.

Attacks, self-will, and faithlessness can be lessons. Regression brings increasing suffering and this conflict becomes more tedious. More effort is put into willingness to use higher technology—and less undoing is needed. Why fly with the wings of a sparrow when you can soar with the wings of a hawk? As we become more aware of being spiritually guided, we gain more confidence in the process of evolution. It makes it even more appealing if we can see the journey as one that has guaranteed a good ending. We are already holy on another level. When we feel the presence of sacred love, we realize it is not a version of conditional love we see in most relationships.

The combination of desperation and the glimpse of consistency in grace helps us move into the unfamiliar with growing trust and an increase in faith. Faithlessness will always limit and attack. Faith removes all limitations and makes us whole. Faithlessness will destroy and separate; faith will unite and heal. As we move forward, we move into the unfamiliar with an uncanny feeling of certainty. Surrender to life! Ready? Try this meditation as an exercise for your thoughts.

Intend to let go of all you know
All the knowledge
All the structure
All the earthly belief systems that define
your present earth-plane reality
Feel what you know dropping away from you.
Surrender to the unknown, free fall into what is.
You cannot find what you do not know in what you do know.
Surrender to what you do not know.
Surrender with the intent of letting the divine guide you.
Surrender and receive what is from a place of open listening.

Die while you live! Be utterly dead. Then do what you please,

All is good.
Shido Munan

Hidden Teachings

Problems are opportunities in work clothes.

Henry J Kaiser

WE REPEAT mistakes to further define the illusion, and mistakes will be strewn throughout our daily lives. They can be repeated until they have taught us their lesson. When I was a child, my mom put together an Easter egg hunt. In each plastic egg, there were candies or pennies. They would watch as we searched in familiar and unique places.

As a spiritual seeker, intent on evolving my consciousness, I was always looking for direction from the divine. It soon became clear that they were not "out there." They were being overlaid on certain experiences, people, and objects from my higher mind or spiritual guides. When my spiritual visions became more powerful and sane, I saw direction and guidance in the mundane and the extreme. In time, and through continued reading and experience, I understood that my lessons were always coming forth for resolution.

Though I had little consciousness around it, karma affected my daily occurrences and relationships. At any time, I could be evolving on a soul level. It became more understandable to look at life on earth as a school and have gratitude for the things, people, and experiences one goes through. Without external objects, the human self could not be reflected.

Without an external backdrop, we might not become aware of the body-self at all. Without others, we would not be likely to dredge up unconscious shadow emotions that find resolution in forgiveness and healing. The loving source was being discovered in my guilt and shame as it became triggered by my actions and relationships.

Thoughts are stored in the body and filled with experiences. These darker aspects are still packed with holy grace and are waiting to be integrated into their roles as change agents to grow the evolutionary self. This integration and the revelatory energy of power help build our personal vessels of divinity on earth. They bring us the fulfillment and peace we long for, and they call to us. This only happens once we put aside victimhood long enough to take responsibility for mistakes that are designed to guide us in the right direction.

For me, an important understanding that arose was that I had to accept that I was not a victim in life. My life was a unique participation in a holy curriculum. I was personally responsible for my choice to incarnate into this school of duality and resistance. When I decided to stop resisting the spiritual perspective, I would be shown my lessons in the mostly hidden teachings. I needed constant reassurances that life was happening for me—not *to* me.

My lower mind or intellect in its evolutionary patterning of self-focus for survival and fear-based references, often saw through the lens of being attacked. The victimhood default must be seen as an obstacle by spiritual seekers and passed by, observed, or ignored. This obstacle is the huge block of wood in the eye. It prevents us from seeing how our lessons unfold in the eternal now of every day.

The tendency to judge creates a dualistic propensity to see beauty as more desirable than ugliness. We feel the vast discrepancy between joy and pain, fulfillment and the unfulfilling and meaningless. The pursuit of the one end of the spectrum is mostly a solid pursuit. The truth that eventually emerges, as we get tired of the inability to escape from this circuitous endeavor, is that our focus must change if we are to increase our spiritual nature and reap the rewards therein.

We are spiritual beings living human experiences to learn and evolve. The pursuit of "what is not" comfortable is imperative. In what we resist and judge as bad, there are teachers cloaked in darkness who smile to us and call for our attention. A great teacher once described it as "a bell ringing for prayer." The valuable lessons are mostly hidden to protect the fragile, ever-shifting self of the personality. These lessons call like sirens to sailors on the sea, and we sometimes fear them because their calls sound and feel like temptation. Giving in to temptation can get us rejected, which is the body-mind's nightmare. That which benevolently calls to us is what most spiritually growing people explore, which is a good start. That which tempts us is usually not explored by most, but it must be explored if we are to balance and heal. All occurrences are informative. All people are teachers of some sort. We must come to know some projected aspect of the body self to move forward toward peace.

That which calls us gently beckons us on the heart and soul level to follow. That which tempts us strokes our egos and moves our bodies to follow.

Notice how quickly and blindly we run toward what calls us. Why do we trust this urge? Notice how quickly and strongly we resist what tempts us. Why do we not trust this urge? In the stillness and fertility of true neutrality, we can clearly see aspects of the self that need to be healed, balanced, and forgiven. If we know what tempts us as clearly as we know what calls us, we increase compassion and become unconditional conduits on earth. There is a secret to integrating this knowledge for ourselves and for others. That which calls us is the same as that which tempts us. It is clothed in a different guise. To know what tempts us in the calling and what calls in the temptation is the goal. Here's a hint: It is all the same: the struggle to evolve.

This important chapter resumes our discussion on the limitations of human perception. If we do not understand that our visions come through the eyes of our past issues and experiences, we presume that our eyes are telling us all that is true. In doing so, we always come back to ourselves when we journey for revelation. This is limiting.

Spiritual people are always being challenged to trust in what they do not know. We presume it is relevant to our growing awareness and evolution as individuals. To let go of the complete reliance on the knowledge we have acquired is a leap of faith. To stop running for more knowledge is to surrender to the ever-present teacher in all. I personally had to acquire more knowledge for curiosity's sake—not revelation.

I came to realize that major steps in my conscious growth just happened. My revelations became much clearer—and so did my understanding of the process of becoming awakened. It came from outside my line of vision and the things I had seen and known. This taught me more faith and trust. I began to understand that revelation and evolution happen when information from outside my previous knowledge collided with my life experience.

People, experiences, and knowledge in the form of books, quotes, and media events spontaneously appeared. I realized that my options for evolution emerged from an infinite source that is both within and without! The obstacle in perception must be constantly observed through neutrality. When we go within, we find variations of the self blocking our perceptions. Pressure, in its undiscovered brilliance, is at hand deep within, but it is the part of us that is plugged into infinite potential in self (and not personality self).

To help with the penchant for my human eyes to obscure the divine knowledge being communicated constantly, I began to journal. I wrote down the dark, resisted thoughts. Their expression allowed for balance that opened my ability to hear the divine clearer and the building of an attitude of unconditionally toward self. I found this to be a major tool in bringing forth the higher self.

The full acceptance and ultimate forgiveness of the dark sides of my psyche became valuable agents of my life and cornerstones of growth. I discussed my feelings of hatred, apathy, revenge, sadness, guilt, shame, fear, and loneliness. I called this dredging of my conscious, preconscious, and unconscious the "wasteland." My teacher explained how this helped express the inherent guilt we all live with.

I realized I was repeating patterns and creating repercussions that zapped my joy and peace—and possibly created physical illness. By expressing my hatred through thoughts, verbally, or in writing—and then seeing its fruitlessness through neutrality—I could get out of real-life drama and stop hurting myself.

By seeing it in writing, without judgment or shame, I could walk away from the harmful patterns. If I tried to heal the revenge attack patterns by hiding the thoughts, I was only hiding from my alleged enemies. I was still harboring hate or vengeance toward them. The battle was still on, and I began to feel out of sync and uncentered.

The wasteland is one tool of externalization that allowed me to allow and forgive my own resistance to being a potentially hateful, vengefully driven being. In a dualistic world, these dark journeys hide forgiveness, surrender, and love. Hidden teachings are seen in everything. You can develop the eyes to see or remain in conflict with the divine teachings gifted through grace. Even though I rarely acted on the dark propensities my mind carried them as ribbons of self. They must be brought to the table and loved for balance.

If the focus of looking at what is happening in our lives has been given the option to be seen as a perfect, timely way of learning, then this spiritual vision is a great helper. When we look at our earthly equipment, we see that we really have donned four bodies. We cannot afford to neglect looking at any of them for lessons of joy or misalignment.

When we are feeling fulfilled emotionally, physically vibrant, or mentally clear, the lesson could be to look at the map. If we are bankrupt spiritually, filled with resentment, and looking for conflict, then the teaching is hidden in projections and attack protocol. Whether through joy, love's fulfillment, love's absence, suffering, or fear, we are being taught to keep our human and spiritual lives on track.

Sickness can bring us into a full view of discordance. It is not necessarily used as a whipping stick, but we must focus on the contention and make other choices concerning things we carry in our minds and neglect physically or emotionally. The emotional body has been the most complicated in my journey.

I have had a penchant for toxic shame, and guilt has motivated my actions since I was young. These dark teachers kept me somewhat in line socially, but they created an inauthenticity and a penchant for self-flogging. This led to having to escape pain before performing any task that was risky. Escape took on many forms—from substance abuse to people pleasing—and all of them reinforced a world flecked with guilt. This became procrastination and the status quo in my life. Healthy shame and appropriate guilt—along with seeing all emotions as teachers and vibrant forms of soul communication—can create rapid growth and loving compassion.

As it became clear that my goal as a spiritual seeker was to become a healing force on earth, I realized that these emotions had to be understood for their divine underbellies. My healing power evolved through the true resolution of guilt, unworthiness, and the revelations I received spiritually. My deeper understanding of the unity of all things rendered my human self integral and needed, not primary.

In guilt and unworthiness, the self is primary and the maintenance of the status quo is justified. This resolution of unworthiness, shame, and guilt gives my life vibrancy today. Suffering and joy are best brought on by relationships as personal teachers. I decided to evolve with willingness, surrender to life's lessons, and open my heart. I knew the highest good was served in every step.

I began to realize that everything on the spiritual journey is divinely placed and inspired. There is no way we can get this journey wrong. There are no wrong turns with eyes wide open. Every step taken is one step closer to spiritual fulfillment, whether it appears to take the traveler forward or backward.

The physical body becomes a perfect reflection of the traveler's path—a perfect map to look for clues to what the traveler must heal. The spiritually minded seeker sees all occurrences as light or dark, all feelings as information, and all people as messengers and perfect mirrors. The body is a gift and a source of valuable information. A damaged heart could mean the spiritual journey is taken on the path of the heart, and love is the theme. Circulatory issues hint to seekers to more clearly define where they are going on their journeys. High blood pressure calls travelers to look at the actions not taken, and diabetes asks travelers to fully explore their general relationship to sweetness.

One can never forget that we will eventually see the divine interior in all things. Through spiritual vision, love is fully and unconditionally theirs—even if the body-mind's default is victimhood, shame, or guilt. With open eyes and receptive hearts, the sacred can be seen in all. The sacred is always working to be seen, and even though one of our four bodies—physical, emotional, mental and spiritual—may be in a dark lesson, faith in the concept that life is happening for us will help us thrive.

> Tragedy is a tool for the living to gain wisdom, not a guide by which to live.
> —Robert F. Kennedy

Unconditionality

When we judge, we have less time for love.

—Saint Teresa of Calcutta

UNCONDITIONAL LOVE is a precious goal and a gift while on earth. The earth school with its laws of cause and effect and dualistic learning sets up many conditions and challenges that serve as a curriculum for learning. This school of dualistic contrast reveals the edges to all of our choices and constantly points to who we are and where we are going on the spiritual journey.

In order to progress in this world of conflict, one needs milestones and indicators to offer direction and feedback. If perception by nature is faulty, we need all types of feedback to assess how we are doing and what is in front of us in order to learn our divinely inspired and supported lessons. One of the most precious of the spiritual technologies presented in this book of love's extension is the healing vessel of unconditionality.

Unconditionality can include unconditional love, but it is more of a soul expression than dualistic stepsister. If there is unconditional love, there must be conditional love as well. This makes it more of a body-mind tool than the being state of unconditionality. These perfect higher mind-energy systems act much like joy and divine love. They have no dualistic counterparts.

For many, the initial practice of unconditionality is intense and complicated due to our misunderstanding of the difference between being and doing. I remember reading about spiritually enlightened beings and advanced teachers being unconditionally loving. That practice did not work for a kid from a struggling family who grew up programed in a completely conditional environment. I was measured by extreme conditions and rewarded when they were met.

Many times, I held on too long in painfully conditional relationships. I was constantly afraid that I would fall short and be rejected. I felt the hell of conditionality while reading about unconditional love or listening to sermons that proclaimed its necessity. If I was to bring out the higher self, I had to learn that the being state of unconditionality was an intentioned mind state that holds all journeys as sacred all the way to their core. Many other journeys were not about love at the core.

I eventually realized that an unexamined life was a constant assessment of conditions and judgments made in hopes of navigating each hurdle adequately. If we are to share hearts of unconditionality, all that happens must be accepted as divinely inspired. I realized that this powerful tool is a state of heart that shows love for all expressions of belief without judgment.

The pain of not reaching the bar of safety in each relationship and the many rules of success I was taught about life were my battlefield of pleasure and pain. I saw a world that reflected this growing belief in conditional existence as a rule. I saw competition as status quo, and rejection and humiliation were the hangmen when I lost. I had such shame and guilt that my mind was a prison house of judgment. I tried to find relief in the world of changing expectations and apparent deceit.

These early experiences were the proving ground for learning spiritual-based technologies. For that, I only have gratitude. Eventually, I was given a great revelation about the nature of dualistic learning. It moved me further onto the path of peace and unconditionality. I realized I could not know what I know unless I experienced its opposite. The ability to learn important concepts like harmony, true neutrality, unconditional love, and non-duality was the gift of living with duality as the predominant law of spiritual evolution.

First and foremost, I had to learn more about self-forgiveness and self-kindness. I tried to fit unconditionality into a multilayered mind that included a belief in unconditional love and self-attack. The body-mind clings to its precious, fragile self-image with stubbornness. These uses for judgment were based on conscious and unconscious conditions I had yet to fully grasp.

I was constantly giving to get and seeking revenge when slighted. I hated people, animals, past events, objects, and future experiences in the now because they did not meet up with expectations. My mind raced to judgment and took pleasure when revenge was observed or meted out. Revenge usually came in the form of angry thoughts or blame. I was not successful in completely shaking conditional thinking, but I soon had two helpful revelations:

- Personally, we cannot require someone to be loving, kind, grateful, or spiritual for you to respect them and call them a friend.
- Socially and professionally, we cannot require kindness or civility to assist someone in healing.

Once using true neutrality became automatic, I could apply it to the voice of conditional responses. I watched as many things throughout my day fell short or went against my conditions. I was not even aware of some of these conditions, but they were exemplified in my reactions to particular people or situations. I could observe how my body-mind needed to constantly define its edges, and solidifying its specialness and separateness through these conditions required constant upkeep. I extended love easily, but I expected love in many forms in return. True neutrality showed me the insanity inherent in this practice and how often it robbed me of the peace found at the threshold of unconditionality.

To make this state of holy mind more prevalent, we can shift our beliefs in love to align to what we are feeling in the "eternal now," adjust our dualistic tendencies to be conditional, and follow these advanced guidelines in the clarity of neutral eyes.

- The intolerable does not exist.
- Everything is exactly as it intended to be.
- Everyone is absolutely perfect in their life's journey.
- Nobody is going anywhere; they have already arrived.
- The demand for gratitude negates the original gesture.
- You are what you see and what you do not.
- You are what you reject and what you do not.
- You are what you believe and what you do not.
- To fear is to resist the divine flow of what is.
- To be fearless is to resist the divine flow of what is.

I began to entertain the thought that love was a personal inheritance and not a bartering tool. I realized that I was love, and the clearer the spiritual mind's voice became with its whisper of inner love, the better my joy and peace experiences became. I learned to extend love without allowing the body mind's fear filled voice for conditions to dictate choices. I could observe my conditionality and choose unconditionality as an option.

That is as far as I have gotten, but my journey could take me further—if that is what surrendering to the divine will bring. All the tools in this section are designed to introduce and deepen our being-ness in unconditionality.

I am healing that conditional voice, and it is growing my inner life in leaps and bounds. The growth of my inner life and the clarity and navigation of these spiritual technologies allows my external life to flow through me for recognition and understanding. I am no longer succumbing to the lure of that which chides me to respond and create karma (as I did in the past). I can manage, address, and resolve what does not flow. I do not need to look back to see the outcome.

I once believed we had to set aside or completely abandon all personal beliefs to be 100 percent unconditional. Whenever I tried it, especially in relationships, I was left feeling vulnerable and anxious. I, like many spiritual seekers, have defined myself by my beliefs, especially the positive ones. One must be very advanced to be able to anchor one's life from one's essence, where all is integrated without need for self. In the pursuit of the type of spiritual fulfillment that comes from living a fully integrated life, we must be conscious and forgiving. The rest will happen if that's the will of the divine. At the higher levels of consciousness, we are not fragmented into beliefs that create conditionality. My teacher made it very clear that I would encounter conflicting lessons as I progressed into the energy of unconditionality. I had to watch the part of myself that presumed that love was the answer in relationships and would be the best response. This led to the realization that I only had a limited grasp on the truth. Perception was still a lens from the past that I was trying to balance. She stated that love was not always the optimal answer, and it was not always the answer for everyone.

Not all journeys are sacred all the way to the core. Not all journeys are about love at the core (despite how they look on the surface). Some are about betrayal and retribution; some are even about cruelty and violence. I had to learn to see all journeys, even those directed by dark teachers, as divinely inspired. The teachings and other tools like tolerance and humility began to develop an aspect of higher mind called *unconditionality*. I began to accept that all of "what is" was gifted to be a lesson and had some divine grace interwoven throughout.

These thoughts may seem paradoxical, but words reveal and conceal. Paradox is meant to resonate healing on a level beyond the intellect. One can watch from above the battlefield and still be in it. One can see clearly from a still point out of the flow of the mundane drama how the human self defines itself. The human self also keeps itself distracted and in a circuitous pattern of meaninglessness events until something moves it to curiosity.

I eventually began to see conditional love as a way to use unconditionality with more meaning. I attempted to embrace all conditions unconditionally, which propelled me to a place I had never dreamed of. By staying aware of my tendency to live conditionally, the consistency of being in the holy mind of unconditionality grew. Imagine feeling your human life from a higher self-perspective that includes everyone, all things, and all events. I began to give without expecting, and I realized that this was being done in a unidirectional expression that required no response to be complete. The human self requires recognition, reward, and remembrance to feel worthy and validated. The higher self is kept active by its use of spiritual technology as a creative factor to live the best life possible. If our birthright is worthiness and the holy self lives in unconditionality, then the earth is a perfect environment to remember this spiritually infused fact.

When the value of your higher self, or anything you express, is known before it is given, then the response is inconsequential to the gesture. At the root, gifts are expressions of unconditional love (unless they are given conditionally).

When we live introspectively, we see aspects of the human self looking for definition through how it is received. My inner child needed healing, and this became easier once I discerned and loved this aspect of self. Duality showed me its edges through contrast and observation when I watched it move in the world. When I focused on healing, my emotions were at his mercy. When he was healed, everything changed.

In this important chapter, one is called to drop judgment completely and accept all. This is as close to unconditional love most of us can get in this life. I accepted that this earth school was about healing the haze of forgetfulness of our divinity. We are here to heal—not be perfect.

We are looking for guidance and love, but we are never defective or broken despite limiting thoughts. You can only be the best person you know how to be in this *eternal now moment*. The use of truth and spiritual technology affect this moment in meaningful ways. Without these tools, we continue to be love. We have the chance to awaken and sacredly live, but our lives will lack meaning.

Here is a teaching story to further illustrate these concepts:

Question: If a man sells his soul for one million dollars so another may
    live, what is spiritual net worth?
Answer: One million dollars.
Question: If a man sells an idea worth nothing for one million dollars,
    what is his spiritual net worth?
Answer: One million dollars.
Question: If a man sells a scheme that promises riches at the expense of
    others, what is spiritual net worth?
Answer: One million dollars.

You are already complete, you just don't know it.

Seungsahn

Handling Wrong Thinking

For significant spiritual growth, only one simple tool is required. It is merely necessary to select any simple principle that is appealing and then proceed with its application, without exception, to every area of your life, both within and without.

—David R. Hawkins, MD, PhD

AN IMPORTANT priority of spiritual searchers in a world of finite form can be what has no end. One can easily see that thinking is a very important part of spiritual and human evolution. How can we obtain abstract spiritual goals and measure things in a realm of constant change and blurry perceptions? We are forced to move in faith and search in darkness for long periods of the journey. This moves us to discuss a priority of focus that can add major measurable progress to one's life.

The monitoring and constant adjustment of wrong-minded thinking is certainly one of the spiritual technologies with the most power. What one does to keep and accomplish higher self-goals increases confidence during the obscure climb out of darkness to whatever calls spiritual people. To distinguish a higher self goal one must look at its "all inclusiveness and win-win strategy."

As you invest in transforming your mind into holy ground, you are investing in your holy self and in those around you. Understanding the higher or holy mind and the use of the mind becomes the sacred ground by which you traverse the challenges that are higher self-designed for evolution. The negotiation of the body-mind in the safety and light of true neutrality gives us the skills to let go of thoughts that can derail us or impede our intention to be a healing force or to gain healing ourselves and keep us in the illusion of separation.

In the light of true neutrality, we see how certain thoughts are linked to patterns of meaningless and distracting choices that create more work for us in the outside world. I began to see that my most measurable growth happened when I felt more confident in being able to be clear on what was wrong thinking. I practiced not making choices based on their nonsense.

Right-minded thinking, whether it comes from the best reasoning of the body-mind or is directly inspired from higher mind, usually has a better effect. It creates less work in the world and less suffering in physical and emotional bodies. We must become skilled bullfighters and avoid the bull of wrong thinking. I heard a story about a great hitter with perfect vision. He could see the stitches on the baseball as it left the pitcher's hand. He saw the ball coming the whole way, and he could hit it at will. This is what is created once we get acclimated to seeing our minds as fertile grounds for soul progression and human evolution.

In graduate school and through my subsequent self-work and reading, I saw the obstacles to feelings of peace more clearly. The biggest and most relentless was my constant self-judgment. I had a gifted, analytical mind, but when it was directed at me and my behavior, analysis gave way to extreme judgment. This judgment spawned guilt, and it reinforced any shame that had been formed. This belief frees the beauty of spiritual vision to observe and sidestep any thoughts that could lead you down a meaningless or destructive path. The divine supports these paths, but why go there when we can focus on the tool of mind management through neutrality? Why not avoid the suffering endured as students of dark teachers? Dark teachers still work toward the same purpose. Why go there?

As my life continued to grow, my spiritual nature became more adept at allowing my outer life to flow through me for recognition and learning. I learned that my body-mind constantly dealt me a hand made up of thoughts that I often found selfish and mean. It became easier to sidestep the lure of that which chided me to respond reactively from both outside and inside.

I saw occasions to hate, judge, cheat, and lie. Thoughts of resentment, doubt, and fear passed through my mind, and they were sifted through for their divine messages. I addressed and resolved what was stuck, and in most cases, I did not look back at the thought, feeling, or lesson that was learned. I am constantly working on letting go of the outcome, but

I believe earth is a place to develop skills and extend them—not be without occasion to grow. It became more apparent once I absorbed the *A Course in Miracles* concept that what is not a love thought is always coming from fear and nothing else.

In understanding this blessed tool of mind maintenance, we should start to be vigilant and informed about the differences between right-mindedness and wrong. These two completely separate neighborhoods have different missions, and they are motivated by different causes. Wrong-mindedness can be recognized by its use of fear and previous beliefs in lack, competition, and limitation. The past rules this house of mind; with its conclusions and errors, it navigates the sacred now with a hand that trembles with fear. This thought house is capable of all anger and fear-based emotional experiences. It is a source of poor choices, physical illness, and karmic consequences.

This dualistic teacher is actually an absence of the higher mind. Its circuitous route of unfulfillment can drive us to be more willing and curious about looking outside of our previous program for comfort. The wrong-minded perspective is a hodgepodge of diversity and conflict, and it strives to value and judge each thought, decision, and person for his or her ability to fulfill a lack that is not capable of eternal fulfillment. This wrong-minded lens keeps us journeying into darkness that only has fleeting rewards. In an earlier chapter, we spoke about the importance of balance in our journeys. This balance helps create oneness of mind, and it helps mitigate the conflict in the body-mind with its penchant for competition and repressed dualistic counterparts. When diversity is recognized, all factors are equally embraced and revered, and there is no lesser or higher choice than in true neutrality, we can have divine clarity. This spiritual vision helps us see through the right mind, allowing us to make wise, reasonable decisions and live as spiritual beings on earth.

When we look at wrong-minded thinking, we see specific rules that need to be addressed. For instance, it became clear that I was willing to cling to thoughts—or they would cling to me. This triggered my victimhood default, and it became clear that it needed to be resolved in some way. I repeatedly let go—only to have it surface in another lesson in another time. This tested my use of surrender and faith as I navigated trusting in divine resolution and the use of right-minded, inspired wisdom to act in the world of form.

I began to realize that my right-minded thoughts were being transmitted through the door of balance and neutrality. My higher spirit self can see in the darkness a lot better than my body-mind can. This revelation inspired me and allowed me to serve from a perspective beyond that which appears to be.

With the right mind in place and the wrong-minded thoughts seen and released, creation was at a new high. The extension of love happened in ways beyond my previous hopes. One might even experience illuminated states where sufficient barriers have been dropped deliberately or unconsciously. This can bring about a greater context and an inner light that is unforgettable. Spiritual seekers are constantly moving past previous stuck points—even if doing so is not obvious. As I began to release beliefs from the past, whether they worked or didn't, my mind truly opened. This new vessel of happy learning was a host to newness. In this newness, I had the increased energy of patience, faith, and clarity. Out of this fertile ground came the following thought concepts that, when used daily and remembered in a timely fashion, accentuated the whole point of mind maintenance. First, we can use the following concepts and phrases:

- let it go
- let go to be free
- dis-identify
- disregard
- irrelevant
- exchange
- make room
- tell self new story
- displace this for that
- lay aside
- ignore
- dismiss
- laugh at
- take lightly
- dispassionately involved

These phrases can be used to allow the flow of wrong-minded thoughts, events, and toxic interactions. The logjam that creates pain is loosened, and the stream of higher consciousness flows with force and divine inspiration. Try out each one—and do so without reserve. Laughing at things or taking them lightly does not minimize the responsibility for something. Instead, laughter relates judgment and provides space so divine messages can be seen in their entirety.

In conclusion, it is wonderful to gain any ground in the house of mind. Once we can balance, allow, and tolerate automatically, peace is more available and more present in our lives. This practice gives us balance that allows our beginning glimpses at oneness and the levels of higher consciousness.

> One who conquers himself is greater than another who conquers a thousand times on the battle field.
>
> Buddha

Sacred Others

We are eagles from one nest, that nest is in our soul.

—Led Zeppelin

As I began to entertain beliefs outside of the traditional, I opened up to truths that had so much more love. I began to feel that truths like "we never die" and "this mess called earth life all ends well" had a better resonance.

I grew up watching television in the sixties when the only things on were commercials and news shows. One particular aspect of the news that still stands out to me was the body count featured on morning segments. The Vietnam War waged on, and I was always so proud that I was on the winning side. We always killed, wounded, and blew up so many more than they did. I played with my GI Joes and had my scripted villains. I coveted those days when I got older because it seemed that I could hate and play at the same time.

I began to see the others were not as predictable as the news, and the atrocities I saw on shows like *Biography* actually had a tether to real life, my real life. My parents had a difficult relationship, and some of the effect was seen in violence. I watched two people who I loved beyond belief physically and emotionally hurt each other in plain sight. I am revisiting this thirty-three-year-old memory only to say that it was during these years that others became real teachers, and I started to see that love and hate could live in the same house—not just on TV. They eventually fell back in love and died seemingly peaceful that their lessons had been learned well. Growing up sensitive and very affected by other people's poor relationship skills, I sought emotional and physical safety from a very young age.

Sacred others teach always and everywhere; they are probably some of the most important tools in spiritual evolution. They have the potential to help awaken our awareness of the both the body-self and our innate holiness. As I got older, I searched for answers to fill the suffering emptiness. My past relationships had a lot to do with how I handled everyone in the present.

Projection is always relevant in relationships. We have relationships with all things in life, but people are the most complicated. Our interaction with careers and objects can be intricate, but our relationships with people continue to penetrate our hearts. That's why our perception or understanding of why people do what they do was of supreme interest. Sacred others are powerful teachers because of the roles they play and the messages they bring.

An angel visited me in a dream and said, "All journeys are divine. If you cannot find love for all others, then you are not seeing their truth."

If a sacred other shows up in my life as any form of teacher—either light or dark—this divine inspiration is a potentially fertile opportunity for balance and healing. The earth is a place to heal the feeling of separation and all the unconscious fear and guilt that was programed into the body-mind. I have learned that others are efficient at highlighting the aspects of the abilities and gifts that are hidden deep within us. My shame and guilt were so deep that, without an external trigger, I was unwilling and unlikely to bring out repressed fears to be healed and gifted skills to be accepted and transformative.

In relationships, others are perfectly able to help us see ourselves and become the transformed. This becoming of the higher spiritually equipped "beingness" makes room for the anointed, holy self by direct intention or as a by-product of a courageous heart that stays devoted to spiritual technology. The higher self has clarity that the body-mind and its eyes do not have.

As with everything, how you receive and integrate what is being taught daily determines how your life unfolds. There is no wrong way to interpret your life's happenstances, but some ways are more enriching. It is imperative that we use spiritual technology (true neutrality, surrender, and humility) as a constant centering practice to deliver us from a limiting and confusing perception.

One must fully understand that vision comes through the eyes of our life experiences. If we assume that our eyes tell us all that is, we will always come back to ourselves as reference—no matter where we journey for revelation. This is limiting, especially in relationships. In relationships, we are constantly being challenged to trust what we do not know and presume it is relevant to who we are and what we are becoming.

Many of us are not versed in phrases like *transference, perception,* and *projection*. We must believe that the body-mind is limited by several factors. It relies on previous programming, desperately seeking answers in search of peace, resolution, or control, which can never be found, fulfilled, or sustained on earth without total surrender to the spiritually powered higher self.

Once we realize that normal thinking and vision are limited, we can discern truth from falsehood. When we use surrender and neutrality to journey with faith in the spiritual mind as a guide, we begin to trust that the journey is on track—even if we feel suffering or joy.

We navigate relationships with two missions in mind. Since a good part of this journey relies on relationships to meet human and spiritual needs, we have to integrate both worlds with compassion.

The spiritual seeker of today is usually a busy householder who has chosen to be in the middle of modern life. We have to find time for spiritual study and practice while meeting the needs of social existence. This dualistic cauldron is perfect for extreme levels of evolution because the amount of interaction is increased, and we are constantly forced out of our comfort zones. There is no escape from our projections because they come from inside our minds and are looking for objects to be shown on. The tendency to see how we are being mirrored in our relationships helps us in several important ways. Whether we accept it or not, we are constantly getting feedback about who we are and how we can become more socially pliable. We have constant opportunities to trigger hidden, repressed obstacles to our spiritual goals.

We are constantly being drawn to people who make us feel good. We assume they are safe havens. I eventually excelled at creating some safe relationships, but I was constantly being challenged to be in relationships that were not comfortable. I realized that thinking of them with respect made these dark beings a must if I was to reach my goal of becoming a fully functional vessel of divine love. Learning in these relationships became a priority, and navigating them as a human was next on the docket to learn. I had used unfulfilling tools like dishonesty, manipulation, escapism, and blame to hide my need for control. In relationships that felt unsafe, I ran. Judgments and resentments stole my peace. My next lesson was integrating the truth that I attracted these beings as curriculum in a school I had designed for my optimal learning.

I practiced coming from the storehouse of my higher self-love to the point where I could stay in pain-filled relationships longer to learn their meaningfulness. You can only do this when the source of love you draw from is more internal then external. I did not physically have to hold onto the toxic social interaction any longer in order to resolve unfinished feelings or manipulate external situations, but still had either revelation or gratitude for the other being no matter what the end circumstances.

Throughout much of my childhood, adolescence, and young adulthood, suffering was the result of one mental and karmic construct: "If the world loves me, I know I am loved." The need for outside love and safety leaves many of us frustrated and angry. I tried to procure love from others who were not always ready or interested in love as an agenda. This trial led to the following revelations:

- Release your enemies to live their own lives.
- Let go of previous relationship battle plans.
- Allow others to not like us.
- Allow yourself to not be friends with everyone.
- We are obligated to love our enemies enough to respect their unique expressions of life.
- Extend all the love you want to anyone—but expect nothing in return. (We expect a return because we are trying to reinforce our own safety and value).

Not all sacred missions are about love. I saw that much of my social energy was spent hiding from the world in shame or manipulating those I loved. When I felt safe or self-loving, it was not anchored in me—but in how the outside world received me. I was also at the mercy of perceiving their reactions to me or my behavior through a lens of extreme guilt and shame. This made perception a closed loop of suffering.

The light teachers in my life were also prevalent and took many forms. They came from coaching relationships, family, and friends. I had a connection to one particular angel. I eventually expanded my relationship circle to clients and other sacred teachers through movies, books, and experiences. Romantic relationships played an extreme part in bringing light and dark together as one. The physical attraction and hormonal feelings of sexuality and the safety of having one special friend who stimulated extreme safety brought hazards of love.

As I became more aware of the self and its darkness through journaling, discussions with my teachers, and prayer, I learned that I am like everyone else. Sacred teachers give us many lessons; it seems that all my hidden darkness began to emerge to be forgiven in relationships. The sacred others closest to me were the greatest mirrors, and I would painfully follow the breadcrumbs back to what seemed like a tortuous uncovering. I was constantly forced to forgive, surrender, and change my mind to believe the pain was perfect for my growth. This allowed me to be more authentic in my relationships and to make better choices in them.

People I came to know and let pass through my life were like seasons. A season is an experience and a time frame that has boundaries and limits. They served growth for a period, and the period was pushed out by the next one. There were no incomplete journeys; all were seen as sacred and holy. No matter how they were dressed—or the nature of the interaction—I could retreat to true neutrality and witness the divinity present in each and every sacred other.

One of the biggest obstacles to seeing others through sacred vision that allows for kindness and growth was the lens of injustice. My body-mind constantly works from a default of "filling and emptying" with others or objects. They are the primary source of my "lack" or my "fulfillment." This tendency was a stubborn leftover from a self that had to constantly define itself at the expense of others and things. "I'm not that." "I have this, and you don't." "I am more." "I am less." The need to use comparison, recognition, remembrance, and reward requires constant vigilance if we are to gain ground spiritually.

I brought this self-darkness to my teacher, and the following truth changed my view of the blockage. I am where I am for fighting to be right. I cannot bear to be treated unjustly. I apparently was missing the point. Injustice is based on the belief that I hold the truth. I realized the trick was that something is either a spiritual truth or a falsity. Anything that defined my self was false or a piece of something. The premise was and always is that there are no half-truths. The human self is a cover or a vessel that must be transcended and set aside. That's why there is no way to perfect it. There is no way out! This brings on the divine holy self. That is where spirit can guide us. There is no injustice to resolve. We cannot really be treated unjustly or even justly if everything is perfect the way it is. Everything serves the highest good. Can we celebrate being treated justly? Watch your answer.

Once we see others from a higher perspective, it becomes easier to navigate and negotiate what seems like two worlds. Through sacred vision, we drop our neediness in relationships. We learn higher self-reliance. We do not idolize and give our power away to human demigods, but we still see their sacred relevance and retain respect for their missions.

Even though all others are unique, we are one and can love or project our issues onto others. They might act in certain ways, but this is meant to teach us and trigger the wisdom below the surface of perception. If you are in a relationship, remember that resonance joins like mind and like soul together. Assume mediocrity—and you will receive dullness. Nothing is done for these people to "know" each other.

If you have issues to be resolved or learn, you are sending out signals right now to a teacher. Light or dark, all teachers have divine inspiration. They have the potential to move you beyond and above the battlefield. Look at the people you are drawing into your life and ask what they are teaching you about you. Once you see it, forgive yourself and change it (if that is your will). We create our relationships on levels we cannot imagine. All are perfect for the greater good!

Everyone is acting in this scene of your life. See the divine light in their eyes. See it in their actions and hear it when they speak. Everyone is playing the divine for you. Watch them and learn the knowingness of spirit and sacred self.

All I Am Not Is All I Am Becoming!

You are braver than you believe, stronger than you seem,
and smarter than you think.

—A.A. Milne

WHEN WE look at this healing paradox, we must first recall the rules of duality. Duality and measurement help us understand where we were, where we are, and where we will go. Without these backdrops, we have little or no reference in the world of form. We have no reference to spiritual reality. We might only see it in our dreams, connect with it by faith, or hear about it through stories.

To proceed in any meaningful direction, we must leverage a map made up of experiences and associated feelings. This gives us invaluable information for fostering hope and curiosity in shadows as we grow in confidence, faith, and surrender.

A talented young man I knew years ago said, "All I am not is all I am becoming." His anxiety drove him to journal and write poetry to pass the time when panic set in. I brought up the notion that his fear was teaching him faith and that he could lessen the physical suffering by reframing the mental experience. We used this concept to conquer many of his misperceptions about his personal, body self, which allowed him to entertain the advent of his higher *self* as a possible consequence of his sufferings. Through the practice of spiritual vision, he was able to see that his healing was in owning, expressing, and releasing old emotions, mental constructs, and expectations that no longer served him.

The lens of spiritual vision transformed his apparent mistakes, failures, and shortcomings into doorways to his best *self*. In other words, his misperceived darkness was just a sign of his true self emerging. He knew, as time went on, that he would have to stay vigilant and not judge himself harshly or wallow in self-pity if he was to see the divine aspect of self, waiting in the wings to be integrated into his life as *self*.

One day, he said he was lazy in school, which had been a pattern since he was young. He was able to realize that he had previously been a great student. He was suffering and lying to convince his parents that he was not wasting their money, and it was too much.

The remembrance of his responsible truth-filled higher *self* called to him to change his behavior. Within one semester, he turned his grades around and felt smart and honest again.

As we venture further into the integration of this motivational technology, we heal our self-reproach in chunks. By seeing problems as gateways to change and mistakes as opportunities to grow, we remind ourselves to always ask what we are learning. Suffering creates curiosity, and curiosity spurs on the willingness to go beyond to places we need to travel if we're to be transformed.

As I progressed on the spiritual ladder of awareness, I relied less on things like ritual and formalized religious practice. I still went to them as tools and viable options to navigate certain lessons—but not in such a fearful, clinging way.

I grew up doing things to feel good. I was undoing any mistake with good deeds and overdoing any fear by buying safety and creating safe barriers to maintain my inner fragile integrity. I did to *be* because when I went inside to pull from my bank account of *being*, all I got were a few shreds of previous doings that somehow met the grade and could be counted on to give me a boost.

At one point, I noticed that I would read all of my army medals, college awards, and write-ups and stare at my graduate diploma in order to feel better on a tough day. I was overlooking—as do many of us who crave peace and oneness—that the *being* who accomplished those things never left and was always present.

I soon realized that I was searching for something more certain and more solid, something that could only be found on a more essential level and beyond what I could have created or changed. I began to see the concept of *being* as I did my nationality. I'm Irish and Italian. I am those things—no matter what I do. My DNA will always be the same—no matter what clothes I wear or what I say.

When I understood this truth, I saw my pursuit of oneness in a different light. I was doing to *be*; I was working at *being*. This led me to kick back and observe. If oneness is a state beyond duality, then it must fully integrate doing and *being* and make it something else entirely. The analogy that came to mind was the union of hydrogen and oxygen to beget water. The effect is a jump in structure, but the original elements are maintained. The human journey has several rules that can't be avoided if one is attempting to evolve. It incorporates finiteness, which is about time, process, measurable growth, separation, boundaries, achievement, and completion. These are all I am not!

As a spiritual being, I live in the infiniteness of the *eternal now*. I live using resonance, unity, expansiveness, and oneness. On a spiritual level, these expressions are my lineage and have *divine grace* as their cohort.

To move to a concept I've been breaching thus far, but that needs clarity now, we have to address the thought of mistakes or what used to be referred to as *sin*. The realization of the illusion of sin became clear when seen through the lens of spiritual vision. Using the healing miracle thought that we never really do anything wrong—we just make mistakes out of ignorance—we have and will do things that lead down dark side roads.

Eventually, all side roads lead to transformation. This whole mistake-forgiveness process has one of the greatest outcomes. Compassion is born out of the integration of conditional and unconditional love. Imagine one of the greatest tools of all being an integration of our worst and best endeavors.

This felt so much better to resonate with than the nonstop shame and guilt vibration. The past is best used as a measurement system to adjust in the now. Shame, guilt, regret, and all other dark teachers in the emotional body are perfect for their mission to alert us to what needs to be observed and changed in the body self and it's mind, but they aren't to be overused or made into a solid belief that limits us. This is prevalent in many spiritual and less spiritually minded people due to the amount of culturally reinforced guilt and punishment in the media and in dysfunctional relationships.

Life unfolds in miraculous ways when we recognize dark emotions as teachers. These teachers help us learn about whom we aren't and point us to where we can hear the divine guidance in the eternal now more clearly. When I respond in harmony to what is in front of me with the intention to embrace and learn more, truth illuminates and peace surrounds. What would compel you to aspire to find inner peace but the knowledge of it and what it isn't?

When I respond to what is in front of me with the intent to change the situation, I'm acting out of impulses generated from dark emotions, assuming what's happening is bad or more painful than trusting that it's *divine will* and being more patient as the lesson unfolds.

When I act out of my own perception and don't use prayer, true neutrality, surrender, and patience, the divine expression becomes blocked. I'm left to fix the problem on the body-mind level. This grows tedious and steals my peace.

My whole journey is constantly a challenge to stay centered in the divine higher mind and surrender to what is. This is a place of movement and growth. As I continue to practice, I'm able to feel and express more divine love. If I was to let go of my own best thinking and doing, what else could I trust?

As time pushed me forward, I discovered that there was a divine purpose in the school of earth that I could hold onto and teach. Life from the body-mind perspective is a battleground of winning and losing—all enacted in the search for self-definition. In fact, the more you lose on earth, the greater your personal strides and the more you learn about who you aren't.

When we begin to awaken as spiritual beings, self-love and forgiveness become our immediate and constant companions. We become the instruments for the awakening of others. This allows our mistakes to become welcomed teachers. Recovering from their undoing is part of the sacredness of the journey. It is not something to fear.

As we move through the transparencies of what we aren't, our perfect divine self makes its grand entrance. When we see what we really are without judgment, then we begin. The past can be used as a measurement tool and a system for being in the now by constantly using divinely inspired choices. When we bless everything, especially our houses, food, meditations, and workplaces, they become sacred.

Our sacred being is found in the vibrancy of the interaction of what is and what isn't (what works and what doesn't work and what I can see and what's still hidden).

We can use our experience and the ability to feel the grace found therein, but this journey of faith calls for a courageous heart. We also get a chance to get a glimpse closer to oneness when we see the higher self as a collective level of consciousness that includes all others. On earth, this is a completely new experience!

If we want to know who we are, then we must pay attention to any experiences primarily with the tool of humility. We must understand that awakening also constitutes a loss of identity, all that was defined as identity up until that point, and all I am not. What is not creates desire and sets in motion your passion and calls in our unique soul expressions to fill the void.

Unless we agree to suffer we cannot be free of suffering.

D.T. Suzuki

Self versus Self

The poor farmer makes weeds; the mediocre farmer makes crops, The skilled farmer makes fertile soil.

Zen saying

IN SELFLESSNESS, in less-ness of self, self is lost. The lost personal/body self is the treasure. The concept of body and intellect self versus holy and higher mind self brings to light the ultimate in dualistic power. If the primary purpose of this world is to teach that we are much more than anything that has to do with death or limits, then we have to have limits to remind us of our unlimited holy selves.

The human heart beats to a finite cadence. The spiritual heart beats to an infinite cadence. When the physical heart skips or adds a beat, there is concern. When the spiritual heart skips or adds a beat, there is growth. You stop where you are, and feel revelations as the new territory comes into view. There is elation in the infiniteness. The beauty of this tool, like all other spiritual technologies, is that it works in a world of paradox and duality, which gives us the freedom and time to strive and evolve at our own paces while we experience the full range of our mortality and divinity.

We need a body to realize we are spirits. The same is true with the self and its divine origin (the higher self). As a sacred self, you first inhabit a self filled with pain and plagued with flaws and misperceptions. Denying human persona or self is like denying our body. Though confusing in the beginning, we become clearer on our spiritual paths.

When we deny one half of humanness or spirituality, confusion is the only result. The miracle is seeing things differently then we soar like eagles. There is truly no escape from the world we see through human eyes and experience in a fleshy body. Once this truth is embraced, we can activate the courageous willingness inherent in higher self to realize that self was always a prison with an open door. You are always finite and infinite in your life on earth. You inhale and exhale. This is how duality teaches. You are more infinite than finite, but you walk the finite path until it ends. There is no escape from it. Finite is the in breath. Infinity is the out breath. What we are never changes, but who we are changes constantly. In order to realize the power inherent in this dualistic interplay, we must understand the lessons of having a human self. There is really no human self, but we use its character like a set of clothing to live in this world. This is due to the premise that all that is real is unchangeable.

The higher self is in communication with an aspect of the self, we call the body self but most people cannot hear or recognize its wisdom. It's like we have an all-knowing guide with us as we live out our daily lives but we rarely do what it takes to make the communication more clear and practical. True wisdom is this voice combined with divine love. It can be accessed through practices like meditation, reading and dream and journal interpretation. The primary goal of the higher self is accomplishing its soul mission. These soul missions are designed to move us forward on the essence level to a place where there is all knowing.

We learn much on the body-mind level, but the higher self—because of its connection to all knowingness accessible on the level of higher mind—will never be satisfied with the finite.These earth missions can bring great pain or pleasure, and they are designed to use time as a way to continue to develop abilities like spiritual vision, divine listening, sacred hearts, and divine wisdom. These abilities are all part of the holiness of the higher self, and they are uniquely designed for each soul.

As the self feels its limits, curiosity grows. The self becomes more willing to use spiritual tools. The holy self is in direct communication with the divine, and it constantly assists through many channels to save time and bring light. The higher self knows no boundaries, and it is not limited by perceptions or distortions. There are no obstacles for the higher self to hurdle—except for the ripeness of its human sidekick (body-self) to believe and hear the messages. The holy self is our right-mindedness, which sees reality without distortion. The higher self has the ability to hear divine guidance clearly, and it also has the desire and skills to repeat the knowledge of the divine clearly to the self and to others in verbal, written word, or practice.

As we become more aware of our greatness, we realize that the source of all our power—love and joy—comes from this transformation. The higher self can go by many names and be felt in many ways. Some people liken the higher self to the Holy Spirit, Jesus, Krishna, an advanced saint, or a teacher. Others liken the higher self to right-mindedness, or a fully actualized intellect. Some say its divine truth, or wisdom. No matter the name, the greatest distinguishing character is that we are not the author of its truth, wisdom, or love. It flows through us and from us into the world for a greater good. On the level of higher self, communication comes from knowingness and not a situation of learning, like the self.

The issue of having a working sidekick self that has a personality and a separate body and a holy self—already in place in a part of our minds and acting like a coach—brings up many interesting thoughts. Clarity becomes the primary lesson as we learn more about how to discern between different aspects of the selves.

A main concept in this book is the full embodiment of higher self as a conscious experience. To become less you and all you is the goal for many seekers. I know this sounds vague, but in the absence of definitions or ways to identify "you" in concepts, the holy you/higher self can emerge. A sense of identity self /body is not a fair substitute for natural identity (holy self). If we can use tools like the neutral witness and meditation and pay attention without adding a concept or worrying about how this "you" is doing, the movement of awakening becomes possible.

Without this clarity, our alignment and pursuit of truths can cause confusion. As I learned more truth and became more adept in the use of humility, it became clear that a large amount of fear resides in our subconscious. The dualistic interplay between different aspects of the self nibbles away at low self-esteem as we allow for higher thoughts which increase our innocence and worthiness to be held and become aware and release the fear we carry in the pain body of self. The body-mind constantly runs programs that are misguided and self-castigating. To complicate matters, in the absence of clarity, the truth you align with could be your own truth—not the absolute or sacred truth. Without clarity, the lens you see through shows you only what you can best bring into focus in the murky field of vision and perception you might have. We must always watch the part of self that says, "This is the way it should be done."

The energy that gives power to the body is the need for fulfillment without the ability to know truth from falsehood as its primary objective. We judge our worth on the outcome of endeavors and others who are incapable of allowing success or giving love. The fear and lack that fuels this energy source push the development and utilization of self into areas that could be nebulous, unclear, or dangerous.

The body-mind picks one path to follow, and it assures itself that this path is the one and only path to take because it serves the self. There are times when the self chooses through so-called spiritual eyes and loses touch with the higher self by becoming its own higher power. The goal is to intertwine the dualistic and karmic lessons of different aspects of the self, trusting in and surrendering to the direction best suited to meet your soul mission. Until we bypass this confusing mess of the body-mind powered, self-clouding voice of self, we must break the bonds and chains of attachment to concepts. If you truly want to live your divinity of self, then be aware and conscious. Pay attention to the present experience in the eternal now.

The observation of the self from any angle other than identification with the body is an invitation for the holy self to enter. Awareness through intention to evolve will keep moving us forward to our inheritance found in the qualities of the holy self. The higher self is all-inclusive, and it will affect every part of your life. Keep in mind that the goal is freedom—until it dawns on you that you are already free. This freedom is not something in the distant future to be earned by painful efforts in the self. It is eternally one's own, and it needs to be used!

It might appear that we are beating the self and winning freedom, but all we are ever doing on that body-mind level is constantly reinforcing that we can never escape. There is no winning over death. Liberation is not an acquisition. It is a matter of courage—the courage of both human and sacred heart and mind to believe you are free already. Act on it.

Once the shift occurs to higher self, the loss of devotion to self is not a result of decision or work. You are no longer interested in its circuitous route to nowhere. This is where "acting as if" works best. Your holy self can become your saintly self if that's your path, just waiting for your full permission and whole belief in its holy welcome! The higher self is the right-minded voice in an impulse-first mechanism called thinking. This body-mind mechanism with all its symbols and identifications longs for the attachments that give it value and safety. The body self is never able to live in certainty because perceptions of these things change. The higher self is the doorway to certainty and invulnerability and is accessed through faith. The following descriptions of self are designed to help with discernment between the two. This is not to enjoy the victory over the lesser, but it can help give more belief to the latter and maybe even stir some gratitude for having a body self.

- The self will imbibe in wasteful indulgences.
- The self will repeat mistakes to define its boundaries and even make it unique.
- The self has many opinions.
- The self creates community through suffering.
- The self separates rather than binds.
- The self sets aside without learning the lesson.
- The self does not trust in the divine impulse.
- The self is constantly learning and feels lack. Through compassion, we sing praises to those who falter. We become aware that they have hit the wall and know where the edge of what the lesson is for them. They now can awaken.

As long as you think self is the real you, your holy self will seem like the sidekick, the fantasy partner, or the spiritual you. The switching of this dynamic is the real healing in these tools. We become tired of their circuitous routes. Through intention into newness, we move to welcome the higher self through prayer, awareness, and other surrender tools, especially true neutrality.

The following abilities become accessible because our new belief unlocks its gifts. First and foremost, the holy self does not strive for safety in a world that changes it only sees the world as a classroom for forgiveness and remembrance of oneness. The self is activated by the pursuit of safety, and it will manipulate for love. When it thinks it is loved, it feels safe.

The higher self is love, and even though the present lesson might look and feel like hell, the higher self always recalls the best lessons to assess the current situation. The higher self does not move with the outside world of good or bad, happy or sad. It knows it is truth beyond thought, yet it is thinking.

The real need all of us have—and a main purpose of this book—is to bring seekers to a self-state that is solid. This certainty is a higher self-generated love that has no conditions, yet it knows how to deal with all conditions. It just has a deep realization of the truth of its being. This is the place where you can access the "peace beyond recognition." It is our destiny to know who we are in loving glory—without demanding recognition of any kind.

Journeying with both selves teaches us who we really are and who we do not want to be. The self lives with a body-voice that constantly critiques our lives. This thought can create so much pain as it triggers the core of our victimhood default and the tendency for self-punishment. We eventually blame it on an internal aspect or external entity. What if we never did anything wrong? In this school of forgiveness and learning, we do things that lead us down dark roads and require us to learn wisdom. This is important as we strive for experiences of our anointed holy self because it is the opposite of self. Self does not have the distortion or the boundaries of self. It is all-inclusive, yet it comes from a perfectly unique perspective. All things are possible with the higher self, and everything is held in wisdom; everything is understood. It is like living in the same neighborhood for fifty years. You will know your way around. There is no more learning because everything is understood.

The holy self resides in complete harmony with the divine. There are no more obstacles. The holy self can teach self when we use our decision-making minds through neutral witnesses and are open to listening. The divine love is the water running through the pipe of our open holy self-minds. This integration of body-mind and soul gives us vibrancy. It is not perfection; it is a life with sacred energy and grace.

The openness we are responsible for must be free of judgment, open, and clear of self-agenda. When wisdom from the higher self is received, it is trusted. This will allow it to manifest in our lives. The holy self is like a big brother or sister who knows the ropes and tries to care for an aspect of the body-mind (intellect) that still holds hollowness, insecurity, and fear.

The last part of this chapter is dedicated to concepts that will bring us closer to living in holy self.

- Acknowledge our concerns that our present self is not giving us fulfillment.
- Do our best to find peace with what is at present, remembering it is still part of a holy evolution.
- Apply our best human wisdom.
- Follow our joy.

- Imagine the hollowness felt (as we let go of body self) in the emptiness of surrender.
- Pay attention between hollowness and the fertile emptiness of surrender.
- Listen for either self in the emptiness.
- Realize hollowness is a less than Zen state, and emptiness opens us up for receptivity.

In conclusion, once we allow the higher self to run the show, we won't forget self and body. We won't be identified with them. Once we see the self clearly, we can carry it around like a pet. We will no longer need to have pride of authorship the body self-craves. We will feel beauty in all of creation.

The analogy that best describes the difference in the selves and the process of spiritual evolution is the story of Michelangelo. He saw a huge piece of marble in a quarry one day, and he immediately envisioned David. The stone is the self with all of its rough edges and mistakes. David is the perfect product, already existing in its potential. Michelangelo chipped away at what was not needed to get to the essence and core of divinity inherent in us all. One must begin to imagine oneself as one who suffers in an earth suit, but that's not the real you. We are only doorways of essence.

The holy or higher self awaits your total belief, like the David awaited his release. Your ability to integrate humanness with a new love contains great power and potential. This potential can be startling at times; it will show itself in many ways, and also not show at all. Be prepared. In duality, we will still be without certainty at times. Desires will take over. On the path to higher self, time slows things down enough to allow for unfolding. We can learn slowly, take in the lessons, and extend them later.

Personal characteristics can be put under the care of body self, but they are powered by an evolutionary energy coming from the body's life force. One can accomplish much with their human learning and imagination, but it will all end. Self creates through extension of holiness itself, and it is the divine spirit that animates it. The self is run by fear, lack, and the need to define itself.

Even through definition and earth fulfillment, we can only glimpse fulfillment and permanence. The holy or self is "whole", and the source of all essential life is our conscious selves. Each soul's holy self looks different as it manifests on earth. How cool! For many, a mini-death is to come—and a mini-birth is to follow. This is the true message of Christmas and Easter.

Behold I do not give lectures on a little charity.
When I give, I give from myself.

Walt Whitman
Circa 1840

Forgiveness as the Bridge

The angry people are the most afraid.

Dr. R. Anthony

In this chapter, we will discuss the power and diversity of the great tool of forgiveness. Some seekers and many spiritual teachers consider this tool to be the most advantageous to the evolutionary process. To begin, we can first discuss a psychological hypothesis that brings lucidity to the secret of the power of forgiveness. The body-mind is never mad at what has happened (due to its reliance on the past). We are only mad at what does not happen.

With careful investigation, it appears as though the body-mind approaches every day and every situation with a preexisting belief about how things should be. This sets the foundation for our judgments. Therefore, our evaluations and resentments are wholly reliant on comparison to conditions being what we expected. This leads itself to many problems in a world of constant change and many variables.

Spiritual truth taken in and integrated can create life-changing miracles of thought. A miracle is a correction—not a creation. If perceived in neutral clarity, it will show time and again that what the body-mind has first perceived is false. It can only be corrected by a source of truth outside our limited, previously learned, self-serving perceptive vision. The miracle undoes errors created by the inherent flaws that perception needs to see what it looks for. The truth can become a miracle if received with open hearts and minds—through the ears of the higher self. The power of forgiveness comes to change mistakes and is seen as justified. Every intention to forgive, regardless of sincerity or degree, brings heaven closer and allows for more clarity and light.

As we look at what causes hatred and resentments, we quickly see that the belief in separation is at the root of the need for forgiveness. In this world, things are broken up into winners and losers. There are gifts for the winners and consequences for the losers.

There are two ways of looking at our lives. One focuses on seeing that our bodies and selves are separated in ways that are irreconcilable. In this vision, we see more separation than union, and a mind-set grows stronger and stronger as it sees separation everywhere. This view of the world as a place where differentness and diversity are rewarded, and reinforced through this reward becomes the default perceptive lens of the human eye. This can be a cause of prejudice, hatred, projection, and revenge.

We naturally feel unsafe in this world because of our identification with the fragility of the body. We sensationalize the roots of this by highlighting the inherent violence and mistakes humankind makes as it climbs the evolutionary ladder to oneness. The "unforgiveness" in this mind-set is impulsive and can become all-encompassing. This type of mind-set automatically assumes that something is wrong. When we assess this mind-set, we see the root of man's inhumanity to fellow man and our major wars and cultural conflicts. In this mind-set or state of mind, we uncover our intolerance of things, people, values, beliefs, and anything else that helps reinforce a self that needs to define itself on a primary and solitary level based on drama, conflict, and opposition.

The issue of separation runs much deeper than expected when we actually judge each other's beliefs or ways of life. This is not a statement about values. It is a merely a restatement of the inherent intolerance built into the body-mind.

On a primitive level of consciousness, one could see that discernment of safety and intention of strangers were needed in our primordial strivings. This evolutionary quality works well in a world that believes in separation and awaits attack. As perception constantly reinforces itself for self-validation, it gets recharged on unconscious and conscious levels quite frequently.

This cloudy premise projected from a subconscious guilt that feels as though we did something wrong somewhere at some time—possibly in our creation myths—is a perfect dualistic counterpart for our new and sacred remedy of forgiveness.

The correction for the unforgiveness mind-set is to shift from this heavier, pain-filled vision, which is fueled by guilty projections, to a vision inspired by the higher self and the divine. The word for this is simply forgiveness. When we forgive on any level, we allow it to be known that—somewhere in our hearts—we no longer choose separation. We return to the natural state of unity consciousness.

When we look at our lives through the mind-set of forgiveness, we begin to heal. When we carry this forgiveness mind-set as our conscious centering, we spread forgiveness throughout the world. Even if we are still feeling victimized, the movement to forgive gives permission to feel truth with greater clarity and scale the ladder of consciousness.

At the top of this forgiveness ladder is the divine belief behind the premise of this book: We are all innocent. All that occurs in our ignorance is divinely inspired, supported, and designed to help us evolve on a soul level. It all ends well. When we use forgiveness, we are touched with grace, and that blessing helps resolve the problem or heal the relationship in real time. One important note about all spiritual technology is that any tool we use is not ours to own. We are not the authors of any of it. There is no one forgiving another, and no country is forgiving another. That would bring such a divinely inspired tool back down into the finite world to be used by the self to reinforce its selfishness and further confirm its elitism.

When you make a decision from the holy self, you are calling in a divine principle to help heal and create conditions for miracles and grace. The holy self is not a finite presence, and it does not take a sense of pride from a finite entity to claim authorship. On the lowest levels of the forgiveness ladder, we believe we are forgiving another. On that level, to be forgiving and of a forgiving mind would contribute to the density of the sense of objective presence because we would or could take credit. In truth, our only part in the use of divine tools is to be a doorway. We must be willing to hold them in either aspects of mind as a sacred act.

The holy self includes all and is forgiving by an illuminated and quintessential light of knowing that includes and powers everything. This is because it sources from wisdom beyond perception. This higher mind knows and orchestrates the inherent purpose behind all that occurs on earth and its divine interior because of its direct connection to the divine.

To begin to understand forgiveness is to be introduced to divine flexibility at its best. We can shift from holding another responsible and playing judge to seeing innocence in all because we believe they don't know what they do sometimes.

One can start with the concept of being a victim and forgive an attacker or withholder. This style initiates a dialogue of forgiveness that can lead to compassion and empathy. One can see an incident as a lesson and forgive because it serves a good purpose. In a job I once had, a very stoic man would not say hello to me or acknowledge my presence at all. We passed by each other in the clinic dozens of times daily. I originally hated and judged him. I labeled him every name in the book—until I realized he was a great teacher of unconditional love. He was allowed to not like me and not see me. If everything was divinely inspired, he was that dark divine teacher I asked for when I decided to become a teacher on earth. He reminded me that the way we think of others determines how we ultimately feel about ourselves. I was being shown that I needed to forgive my own unfriendliness and coldness—even though I am sure my overzealous body-mind would tell me that I am so much more holy. Perhaps I am not if he showed up to teach me! To grow in the awareness and power of the forgiveness mind means that you can be attacked at any time, and the attacks are perfect.

As I evolve, it becomes harder to feel my hatred or anger and immediately retaliate. Many seekers will grapple with this concept. One must accept one's demons in order to overcome them. As I was filled with more faith, I could do deeper self-searching and healing. I began using surrender and putting on a forgiveness mind. I continued to watch with neutral eyes that were still invested in seeing and feeling clearly and neutrally. It is an act of arrogance to remain a spiritual seeker, judging the path of others and pitying them or blessing them. I at times fell into this body mind trick and used my spirituality to hide from the depth of my human lessons. I specifically recall feeling above others because "I had the way".

I forgot to forgive my human self, and in doing so, I forgot to allow compassion for other humans who were feeling the pain of this world. How else was I going to remember my own inner child who was prone to being wounded? In the beginning, I forgave from every angle I could because I had such low self-esteem. I was really buying safety from feelings I felt were intolerable. I am now able to integrate my human needs to feel hurt, anger, and resentment with spiritual truth, which allows me to see that they are teachers for me. They are not attacking me. When one abides in the mind of forgiveness, one must eventually discern how to stay safe socially while letting go of the tendency to accumulate resentments. This takes time and leaves us vulnerable. During this stage, we must have courageous hearts and trust the process.

As I progressed in my understanding of forgiveness through practice and trust, I realized verbal attacks from others provided opportunities for progression through forgiveness. Salvation showed itself as the undoing of the aspect of self that lives intolerantly as a choice maker. To be annihilated over and over again without retaliation will loosen the self that takes itself too seriously.

In the following chapters, we can view joy as a gift from the right use of all tools, especially forgiveness. Forgiveness makes places, occurrences, and people holy.

Forgiveness has many levels within its healing structure. We can forgive an object or situation like a person or an injury. We can forgive the intention for an attack, a slight, or an oversight. We can forgive ignorance and write it off as fate or chance. We must eventually accept the wound and forgive the self. The trick to healing by using this divine tool is to forgive it all. Every layer must be whitewashed with a new story. You must let go of weaponry.

When I refer to weaponry, I mean attacking thoughts and all forms of retaliatory plans or action held in the mind or acted out. Lessons have no relevance if we carry the battle in our mind and await a new symbol with which to fight. In some cases, this could actually attract a new adversary, which would force us to start over again.

Forgiveness is the bridge to true healing. True healing is not always seen in forgetting, but it encompasses a passionate view of the person, event, or self-action that allows the full complement of understanding and transformation to occur. To understand, and release the pain of un-forgiveness, all things must be forgiven. Once they are understood, integration can occur. This is the formula for evolution or transformation.

In the case of the victim-abuser scenario, it is important that neither one remains in the role of good nor evil. When you trust the lesson of your attacker, you give more trust to yourself. You gain back the higher self/self-love that was lost as victim or abuser. To be a victim is to diminish ourselves despite the popular belief in powerlessness. Famous accounts of abuse have created courageousness and soul expressions of light. A good example of this can be found in Viktor Frankl's *Man's Search for Meaning*.

The process of learning forgiveness through relationships can be confusing. It is especially hard for spiritually based thinkers with good intentions and strong wills to forgive on deeper levels—and remain clear about how to proceed in relationships.

We cannot tolerate repeated abusive behavior when we are listening to our right minds and seeing things from the witness viewpoint. We can always attach prayer and compassion, but there will be times when we must move on or let go of a toxic person. This person no longer serves the divine purpose, and it is our mission to navigate out of the drama.

To forgive is to move out of the part of the body-mind that craves conflict and creates drama. Even when we feel the fear that immobilizes us—and we have no clue how to resolve the social issues between people—we can forgive by changing our perspectives about them. Any heavy thoughts we carry about others weigh us down and reinforce our own hatred of self and feelings of separation and loneliness.

If we choose to focus on healing a relationship or situation, we must come to the realization that there is never a victim or attacker present. Carrying around this heavy energy causes blame and thoughts of revenge. Watch these toxic expressions and—like a skilled bullfighter who is fully aware of the bull's power—allow them to pass by. Observe their style.

Another hint that helps with forgiveness is the understanding of time. If it is in the past, then you are carrying it into the present because the lesson hasn't been learned yet. We are always living in the eternal now. Do not forget to rest when you need clarity or a thought that works. You and everyone else are innocent. To carry guilt is to build it up—no matter how long ago the guilt was born. Guilt can help us live productive lives on earth, but when it becomes a state of mind, we become dangerous to ourselves and others.

If we are always doing our best in the eyes of the divine, we can never do anything sinful or wrong. We will make mistakes and wander down dark roads, but choosing forgiveness can rectify them. No one has sinned; we all are just called to learn.

> The fragrance of the violet sheds its scent on the heel that crushed it.
>
> —Mark Twain

Listening to Your Life

Every minute of life carries with it miraculous value and it is a face of eternal youth.

Albert Camus
Circa 1930

A FRIEND once said that if I opened up a holy book to any passage, it would be the one I needed to hear. This set in motion a very wonderful pastime that I eventually began to teach. If the divine is in everything and is everywhere, then messages can come in any form and at any time. If we can release agendas, outcomes, and self-centered goals—and not put out into the world what we want to see, hear, or experience—we can be in communion regularly with presence and progress on the path with greater joy and wonder.

Earlier in this book, we discussed the concept of light and dark teachers as holy others who help on the way to awakening. People are perfect mirrors of dark and light. Our answers are always being given, and our loving creative source is in constant communion with us. To truly grasp this mind-blowing concept, one must at least begin to understand how this shows such worthiness. It reaffirms our divine heritage over and over again.

The first concept that will help make this clearer is looking beyond the mundane happenings of daily life to the abstract. To not focus on content and meditate on context gives us fertile ground. Ordinary life is never just ordinary. The sacred path actually starts when we are curious about where the divine resides on a daily level. This etheric quality is the core of the sacredness in our lives. The quintessence and illuminating love that creates all things and occurrences is where this divine message can be seen, heard, and reverenced. We awaken slowly on earth to the divine holy self. The beauty of time is best seen since it allows the divinity unique in all things to unfold slowly. We can see it over and over and feel the love. Many of us curse time and live impatiently, but if we realize how helpful it really is to have multiple chances and choices, we would be more grateful.

The more we look at our lives on earth as energized and supported by a divine source, no matter what its name, our perceptions can change to spiritual visions. This evolutionary rung on the ladder of consciousness is the restoration of awareness of the inheritance of our holiness. This occurrence brings clarity to our awareness by being able to see divinity reflected in all things as we experience them.

Once we set our intentions to evolve on a spiritual level, the soul begins to bring new abilities into play. The ability to see the blessed synchronicity in nature or the actions of others energizes curiosity to learn more and become transformed through the pursuit of truth. This concept takes some getting used to since we are used to focusing on the dark end of the dualistic aspect of life's travails. Imagine the earth as a holy school with a great outcome. It has the ability to nurture us and help in our daily awakenings—no matter what life seems to be showing.

What if we embrace and grow into a person who strives to listen and receive guidance mainly from higher mind. Will we become more accustomed to its blessings? I envision a time when there is no duality, all is of equal relevance, and all is relevant and inconsequential at the same time. There is no learning here because learning depends on time. We are thinking from a source beyond, and in this beyond, everything is known.

The place of beyond is a goal for spiritual seekers. The mind is a reference point, and we use tools like neutral witness and forgiveness. Our understanding of the earthly rules of cause and effect and duality enhances surrender. Through this fearless perspective, we can see all that happens on earth as a means to evolution. This beyond requires dedication and faith that allows the truth to be communicated in all ways and through all things.

A small child from next door noticed three crows on the wire above our yard. He asked, "What are they saying, Dan?"

I immediately went to an animal totem book and looked up the significance of crows. As it turns out, crows were messengers and harbingers of creation. The following day, he told his teacher that he was feeling very creative and molded a sculpture that I still have twenty years later. That sculpture still inspires me. He still asks me to look up all significant animals he sees in dreams or animals that stand out to him throughout his day. I love how nature—especially all things that move and catch our attention—is a constant gift of communication. Imagine seeing all that happens and everything that comes into sight as part of ongoing communion.

At work, some colleagues ran out to tell me there was a family of ladybugs by the window. I counted their spots and explained the nature of grace to those who would listen. We talked about it being a lucky day. I live this truth daily and spend my day in communion—no matter where I am. When I am centered, numbers appear on mailboxes. I look them up in my pocket numerology book. Each number has a message, especially if it comes in a dream or keeps showing up in numerous places. My higher self speaks constantly and lovingly through my daily interactions. Even though I miss the messages most times, they show up again. That is what love does, right? My higher self is always saying, "I am here! Notice me!"

The previous tools are helpful because they can act like refresh buttons that clear the clouds of perception and allow clarity to reign. This level of living consciously helps create constant reinforcement of our divine heritage and our connection—despite constant trips back into body-mind for alleged comfort allured by temptation and insecurity. The body-mind feels separated and will attempt to reinforce this illusion. I ignore my self-ignorance when I am conscious and feel connected in every way. My occasional feelings of separation from the divine also create a desire for surrender and reinforce my compassion to the plight of humanity as it strives to overcome its loneliness.

When I was vigilant and centered, I was able to hear the lyrics to old songs more clearly. The lyrics were relevant to what I was going through. Songs are a perfect way to listen to divine messages because the vibration is literal and moving. This helps us remember better than mere words. I listened to the group Yes for two years straight, getting all I could from the spiritually inspired lyrics. After thirty years, I realized some of the lyrics were different than I had perceived them. They were so much deeper. I guess I was not ready to receive their depth yet.

This brings up an important issue about levels of preparation. Being ripe for truth also played a part when I read certain books. I arrogantly thought I ingested the wisdom in these masterpieces, but after reading them several times, the books contained completely different messages. It appeared as if a different person was reading the same books.

When I was ready to receive the messages, I began to see that some lessons come out of sequence. In those times, my spiritual maturity blocked or witnessed the truths conveyed. I also became aware that living in a material world can preoccupy and insulate us from change and growth.

As I am writing, my excitement is charging the words. I cannot wait to share them with readers. For the soul, human life is all good. It is all for us, and love is inside and around us constantly if we persist in looking, listening, and opening our hearts.

A wonderful friend told me that prayer was useful to her because of its clearing effect. She used prayer as a centering tool so she could be more aware of the holiness in her mundane life. She connected to the infinite source of the earth to release all heavy and challenging things. She was transformed by walking on the beach, rolling in the grass, and looking at the sky at night. Releasing all things to spirit brought wonderful lessons into the wake of what was released. She lived with both feet in this world, and she surrendered all conflicting energy into the creative energy source of nature. Energy is never lost; it is just transformed. Many seekers who do yoga and meditate know how to release negative energy through the vessel of the body, which brings good physical and spiritual health.

The earth constantly calls us to breathe in its gifts and breathe out that which does not serve us. As we release that which does not serve us into the earth, we receive what helps us grow and maintain an inner light. We are of the earth, learning through duality and cause and effect. We do not know what we need until we lose it. This is the way of the earth; it is how earth teaches. In loss or the absence of inner peace, we realize what we need. The sacredness on earth can help us evolve with more peace if we maintain centered and clear minds.

In what is painful or fulfilling, the information that is needed can be seen and recognized. The sacred is speaking in your life but might not be visible. Integrate the two and connect with faith to the infinite source.

Once we become more comfortable with meditation and/or contemplation, we can learn valuable lessons quicker and with less suffering. If these practices aren't comfortable, try to find some quiet or stillness. These tools will help us decipher the daily messages. I go to holy others in conversation to get other takes on messages or dreams.

Use everything since your devotion fuels the quest to hear your beloved source communicate daily and nightly.

A big clue to staying conscious as we keep vigilant for communion messages is the use and control of guilt and shame. When these two body-mind default mechanisms become dominant parts of self and rule the mind, they block divine messages. They are not to be obliterated. Some spiritual seekers believe these tools are the measure of success in holiness. The full understanding of their lessons is important.

Guilt and shame are dark divine teachers if used in the right mind. These emotional states keep your life on track in specific situations. If they dominate morning to night, they must be resolved and integrated. I used truth and prayer with this.

One of the most precious truths states that no journeys are incomplete. All journeys are revered. All souls incarnate for the continuation of specific spiritual missions. This book is about realizing that the earth is a benevolent school in which only love really exists (despite its appearances). Spiritual vision opens up the ability to see how all occurrences—even ones deemed sad, dark, and cruel—play a part in our perfect awakening on many levels. How can we really know that dark lessons aren't exactly what is called for at that time to evolve?

All information that breaks through perception, especially integration and spiritual truth, is a form of creation. All that occurs or shows itself can be considered like food to the digestive system. Digesting food is unconscious; digesting knowledge is intentional and creates personal growth. Digesting spiritual truths creates enlightenment! Many seekers love learning through reading or wise teachers. It serves them and should be utilized until they are ready to get the egg directly from the hen. We all have our own unique spiritual wisdom, and it is a wonderful uncovering as we progress.

Higher self-revelation—the transformative movements that change everything—cannot be touched if spiritual digestion is not accomplished. Digestion makes spiritual evolution personal. Spiritual seekers must delve deeply into their journeys and travel with trust. It can be frightening to go where no human seeker has gone before. The trips back and forth into the body-mind and character weapons are actually blessed learning opportunities. We must be able to return to the familiar; many people quit at crucial times.

In summary, look into your life: the colors you like and dislike, the books you read and hate, the dreams that come and the times that are without dreams, and the people who are sent with compassion or toxicity. They all will teach us. They all are divinely sent, blessed, and perfect for your evolution on earth. As with everything, how they are received and integrated determines how meaningful the communion is.

You must be able to connect to open listening through an open heart and spirit to see, hear, and feel wisdom. This will allow you to receive wisdom at the level of your divine higher mind, which is directly connected to unity consciousness.

The divine mind is a step higher in vibration than the physical mind. You must be open, clear, and free of judgments. Do not attach judgments to what you receive. If you need help, ask for personal guidance through a book, a teacher, animal totem or a dream. Your faith in the mechanism of the guidance matters most.

Allow and abide by the message or wisdom received as you watch it manifest in your life. Do not get caught on content—and stay on context. Wisdom will never misguide you, but you may not understand it in the moment. At a later date and time, you may come to understand the wisdom you have received. Allow wisdom in any form to guide you! You are a precious child of the divine!

Autobiography in Five Chapters
Portia Nelson

I

I walk down the street. There is a deep hole in the sidewalk.
I fall in.
I am lost … I am helpless.
It isn't my fault.
It takes me forever to find a way out.

II

I walk down the same street. There is a deep hole in the sidewalk.
I pretend I don't see it.
I fall in again.
I can't believe I am in the same place, but it isn't my fault.
It still takes a long time to get out.

III

I walk down the same street. There is a deep hole in the sidewalk.
I see it is still there.
I still fall in … it's a habit.
I know where I am.
It is my fault.
It still takes a long time to get out.

IV

I walk down the same street. There is a deep hole in the sidewalk.
I walk around it.

V

I walk down another street.

Courageous Heart

Courage is grace under pressure.

—Ernest Hemingway

THE TOOL of a courageous heart is gifted. The process begins with surrendering to life on earth with eyes and hearts open. This first step—like with most spiritual technology—brings forth great fear because it requires letting go of existing coping mechanisms. This is like shedding our skin and being vulnerable to the elements. We are actually in the process of losing ourselves to find the inner peace and spiritually evolved gifts in the greater higher self. To many who dare to go beyond our existing boundaries of the finite self—with its limited perception and programmed mind—anything new brings anxiety.

Imagine the courage it takes to feel more me and less me, less fragmented and more whole. It is not one of the most automatic or easiest things to do, especially when challenged to label something or bring it from a past that only exists in memories. Keeping old concepts appears safe in the beginning. At times, it is needed, but the problem with doing this old trick is that it halts our lessons and stops our growth. When I control the outcome, I receive exactly what I create. Repeating outcomes not what is gifted to me in the newness of the yes of surrender. The action required to manage this newness stands in the wisdom of your heart with unfathomable faith and a commitment to be fully in what is happening at that time.

As seekers who are welcoming the courageous heart, the goal is to say yes to our lives to the best of our abilities. We can do this in any way that is comfortable. Prayer, church, self-help, yoga, and meditation are only a few methods. When we begin to open the door to this powerful energy, we often have feet in both worlds. We open the eyes to the new and allow ourselves to evolve at our own paces while holding onto old choices that feel comfortable even if they were fruitless.

We get to decide what meets our needs by comparing outdated knowledge bases and building the courage to move into that newness that can help us evolve. Evolution requires you to be other than you are in this moment—and other than you will be in the next

If we stay too safe in worn-out patterns like denial or self-castigating thoughts, we might become physically sick. We can use physical illnesses to grow courageous hearts. I have seen many people fight cancer and other serious illnesses with a courage that I am blessed to behold. Once we begin the spiritual path, it pulls us forward in an assortment of ways. That's where the courage is needed most.

When we use tools like surrender and become more tuned to our divine eyes and ears, our awareness of all divine options improves. The lessons on earth are not easy. Consider the lessons humility forces you to learn. You are not equal to those you need at times (due to your dependency on them).

We must see others as divine placeholders. When we trust that we are not victims, duality will cease to offer its sharp and tender conflict. The courageous heart allows us to move past rigidity. The human heart is always caught up in the lessons of duality, and it struggles with the unfamiliar. As our courage grows, we can move down the spiritual path. This version of the spiritual heart feels deeper in a vibrational way, and courage is needed to hold its truths.

Everything on the spiritual journey is divinely placed and inspired. Even though we cannot get the journey wrong, it sure feels like we can. It became evident to me that you can thrive within the storm. You can be buffeted by the most vicious winds and the most violent repercussions and still see them meaningfully. This is the gift of the courageous heart. As the strength of this grace-filled tool embodies you and makes a cocoon around you, your job is to sharpen your ability to listen to your heart and the wisdom of its higher vibrational language.

The law of duality plays a big part as a teacher on earth. On the path of duality, we can only know the best choices in contrast to the worst. We call them "good" in contrast to what we call "bad." To move to the higher vibrational levels of heart, we must balance and become aware of the human heart. The human heart is as vulnerable as a moth without wings. The courageous heart is as impenetrable as a warrior's shield. The human heart can die empty and defeated. The courageous heart can die blazing with light. The heart can live without reason. The courageous heart can live with great purpose. The heart is love and light. The human heart is capable of hate and darkness. The human heart has divine gifts. It is the first doorway into the spiritual realms and sacred love. The human heart is the home of duality. It is an important earth-plane experience. In the human heart, there is always the choice of love or hate, communion or separation, light or darkness. All choices hold the potential for growth. We choose. We walk.

It takes great courage to do many things on earth, especially things that relate to the body or relationships. Once we have consciously taken on the vessel of the courageous heart, we can learn to face the most fragile situations. We can emerge as leaders of compassionate choice. We are gifted through human devotion to self and others, and spiritual work allows us the opportunity to awaken the courageous heart. The human self can act like a stunt double by helping us prepare for the entrance of the higher self. The courageous heart is an integration of the sacred heart and the best parts of the human heart. The gift of grace highlights that all is sacred because we are all from the same divine source at heart.

The higher vibrational version of the human heart allows us to go beyond our previous limits. This heart does not have the tendency to give into fear like the human heart, and it has the wisdom of higher self to help us discern our choices. The spiritual heart holds the love of all, of everything, and of everyone. In this vibrational level there is no dualism or split intentions. There is only oneness.

Love is absolutely unconditional. There are no exceptions. Having a true spiritual intention ignites the spiritual heart, which acts as a gateway to the gift of the courageous heart. The divine heart cherishes all it touches. There is nothing to forgive. There is nothing to explain. The courageous heart is part of the gateway that welcomes divine love to the earthly plane.

When we look at the basics of courage, we see that the mind-set helps us face difficulty or danger with wisdom. It utilizes fear and initiates wise action, bravery, and valor. When we look at this vibrational energy as a color, we see a vibrant red that runs through your energy system. It holds us upright, present, and clear when we feel uncentered and misaligned.

If we are using the courageous heart as a growth technology, there are many things to consider and many questions to ask. Most of us struggle with the "others" in our lives. Even though we allow courage to be present, we must still have self-love and use wisdom to live on earth. We should never let toxicity rule our lives. With the tools described in this book, we must clear a path through the debris of many storms.

Even when our struggles have been jettisoned from our daily lives and thoughts, and they no longer dash through our minds and emotions, we must ask ourselves whether we have the courage to go into the black hole of the self to grow more. Can we let go of the victimhood that blocks growth? If we look deeply at courage, we see how it is linked with honesty. Can we ask the right questions with courageous hearts?

- Is there something I have chosen not to see in the past that I can see now?
- Who can I speak to or rely on for support now?
- What resources are available to me to process my feelings?
- How is my fear leading me to my inner wisdom?

With courage, we can move through the human experience. The struggle is to evolve through self and fully be. The spiritual experience—when seen clearly—observes all human experience through the neutral witness with a courageous heart to inspire harmony and unconditional love. The spiritual journey is taken mostly by surrendering the belief in inevitability (something bad will happen) and separation (source is somewhere else) that dominates the body-mind and embraces faith as a new guide and direction. The light of the courageous heart can lead the way.

In summary, one can easily see through personal, local, and global experience that life in a realm that has duality and cause and effect as teachers is going to be challenging. Spiritual seekers eventually come to the realization that coming to this realm is not a punishment, despite how it feels, and that divinity is all around us.

The beauty of spiritual technologies and our persistence in using them give us inner peace, which resonates as a loving extension for the greater good. We must strive daily to see the divine interior being revealed in all that occurs. We must let our courageous hearts guide us as often as possible, not the body-mind. The body-mind can easily turn up the volume of fear and doubt in any situation we encounter.

> It [heart] participates more strongly in what is happening in the depths of the soul because it feels the link between the body and soul more clearly than any other part.

—Edith Stein

Joy

I only wanted to have some fun.

—Led Zeppelin

As we progress spiritually and naturally awaken to more practical truths through their integration into daily life, we have a wider array of thought choices. One helpful thought choice is that spiritual tools are functionally designed to help us be conduits of joy on earth. We can only choose this conduit role once we have taken an honest look at the remaining specks of darkness that block the full awareness of love's presence from coming into our minds. The biggest of these is a poor self-image.

Higher self-love is the starting point of the lives we are meant to live. Higher self-love is the acknowledgement that the only source of love comes from inside the recognition of our innate divinity. Once we've healed this misperception, our true purpose in life can express the uniqueness that defines us with joy. Our behavior on earth can be broken into two dynamics. We are either calling out for love or extending it with joy.

I began this section with a discussion on love's presence to bring attention to the conditions needed for joy's recognition. I still haven't been able to sustain joy. This chapter is a treatise on how to move closer to allowing joy to regain its role on the sacred journey. It is not a celebration of its full arrival. I am writing this chapter as someone on the path alongside you. When I was actively working, I would take the patients outside at eleven o'clock to watch the three-year-olds from the day care center playing on the swings. I attempted to show us how joy could look and remind our souls of their innate qualities.

Love is always joy's messenger. I was so much better at giving love than allowing joy. The higher mind that serves the spirit is at peace and is filled with joy. Once we allow ourselves to bring wisdom and use it in our movement in the world of form, self-esteem and efficacy increase.

We can begin to know the truths that we were not ready to handle in the beginning of the journey toward peace.

The loving source wills us to have joy as a regular experience in our lives. It is the marrow of love in its purest form. Pure love has no fear, and without fear, there is only love. It is actually humankind's purpose to be living examples of joy on earth. As I recognized my power as a healer, I spoke with contagious joy. I pulled people to my words. I realized that joy had energy of its own. I began to look at joy as a spiritual tool. Prior to that recognition, I included joy in human feelings like happiness, contentment, and excitement.

As our relationship with the sacred energy of joy unfolds, we realize it has no dualistic correlate. Happiness has unhappiness, contentment has discontentment, and excitement has dullness. Joy is its own gift.

As teachers of divine love, we are called to bring joy—in its authenticity—through our actions, works, and lives. It's like a recruitment poster for the spiritual journey. No one wants to follow a sullen seeker or teacher. Joy is an attribute of love and extends a sacred invitation to grow. It shares a glimpse of the reward if we do. Joy as love is our inheritance as divine beings, and this precious condition is a treasure when the work to uncover the holy self is done.

Joy is an aspect of sacred love. It is the natural state of being at the soul level in the same way nationality is on the physical level. The soul is pure joy at the essence level, but it is rarely experienced or held onto because the concept of higher self is filtered through misconception, pain, trauma, and lack. We call this "the past." Some lives are actually tortuous, and even though this can set the table for joy in a dualistic turnaround, these tortuous lives seem hopeless and joyless. This misperception of body consciousness can alter the free flow of joy in our lives.

Joy cannot be altered, but it can be controlled or squelched in extreme conditions. Joy is everlasting and as infinite as unconditional love. It is universal and timeless. Joy can be suppressed, but it can bubble forth or burst out of its containment in any circumstances.

At some point, one will revert to joy and respond with a smile or humor. This concept is best represented in Mary Shelley's *Frankenstein* when the monster smiles after being handed a daisy by a child. The human spirit is joy. It must return to itself. It is who we are! We can allow the selves to be joyful. Since it is our natural state on a spiritual level, it pulls us higher when we allow the embrace of the anointed holy self to grow. It's like what red blood cells are to blood. Joy is the essence of divine love. To understand that joy has no dualistic opposite is to realize its power. It never becomes mitigated, and it only brings extreme light. Joy flows like a warm morning light into the most hidden recesses of life. This light can travel unfettered around corners, underground, through water, and into the epicenter of life. When expressed, joy washes through life, affecting everything it touches. The touch of joy is uplifting. It inspires, enriches, and is felt like no other dualistic emotional vibration. One can choose to receive joy or not. Not received, joy travels on. Unhappiness may be felt. Stasis will continue, and hope will not grow. Joy can feed hope like no other emotion can. Its vibration germinates the seeds of hope as they await stimulation.

One can choose to receive joy, and it can be felt in any way the individual allows: happiness, bliss, peace, or joy. Receipt of joy prompts movement and the blossoming of hope. Life runs on whatever is chosen by the individual, and this is divinely inspired. The fuel of life is chosen on the soul level, and our daily choices bring them into our lives.

There is no choice more wise or meaningful than the one that best serves. Joy, depression, and suffering are all choices. They teach and help in the evolution of being on earth. Dualistic choices like suffering can only be understood in contrasts. Our powerful dark teachers can pave the way for the acceptance of joy.

Embracing joy is a matter of personal preference. This does not mean unhappiness is always the person's preference. Unhappiness can be a default setting in a life that brings forth suffering, but it is meant to be healed. The opposite of happiness is unhappiness, but there is no opposite of joy. It is an expression of the divine principle. It is like the premise that there is no opposite of light; absence of light is darkness. Similarly, there is no opposite of heat; its absence is cold.

When we center ourselves and connect to the full expression of what is brought to our lives in the moment, we can be the light of joy in its purity. On days when we are scattered and misaligned, we are still the light of joy, but not its purity. We have chosen to follow joy or suffering, and we are vibrantly expressing all the gray areas in between. Welcome to the sacred experience of the earth school.

The light of joy is clear when we are in easy, open relationships with all that is. We trust that everything and everyone in our lives is divinely inspired and sent. As spiritual seekers, we can choose to bring joy deep inside our beingness. It can be perfectly expressed out of the baseline of who we are. When we are operating in our most desired, vibrant way, joy manifests in spirituality as infinite kindness and compassion for everyone we meet. When our intent is joy and the conditions are right, others can feel our intent. They want to align with our purpose. Joy calls them to align with itself. If their soul expression at that time does not call them to align with joy, they might find our expression of joy uncomfortable and not want to align with it. This can express itself in many forms, and it is always a forgiveness opportunity for us. When we are not joyful, we are not hurting anyone. We are simply not sharing joy. Joy is powerful and can affect others in a number of ways—just like the other divine principles in this book.

The power of joy has expressed its healing power in my life over the years:

- Joy clears the mental palette, allowing decisions to be made that serve the highest good.
- Joy clears the emotional palette, allowing states of being that serve the highest good.
- Joy clears the spiritual palette, allowing the soul to clearly express what it needs for fulfillment to be felt.

Joy is a way and a meaningful choice, but be cautious. To believe joy can be—or should be—experienced in everyone's life is arrogant and ignorant. Being around animals and children or doing pastimes that are purposeful or mundane can also serve to increase your vibration of joy. It serves all humanity to bring joy into the world. The soul calls for what it needs. When it feels fulfilled, there is joy—no matter what it has called for. The following personal declarations awaken inner joy:

- I awaken the higher self-love gifted to me, intending for it to fill my energy field and my life in ways greater and deeper than I have ever experienced!
- The inner joy embedded within higher self-love greets me.
- A smile rises up from within me and fills my life.
- I feel filled to overflowing.
- I allow my inner joy to guide me.
- I am the joy I feel!

I hope joy and love are with us often. Some others—even though they are perfect in our lives—might have completely different views. The things we do as seekers to grow on earth might seem tedious, and the body's limited and fleeting capacity to hold joy can be felt and used in relationships in an attempt to energize them.

Once we become more familiar with joy's vibration, it can give our activities extra energy—and joy can remove all obstacles to healing.

Joy is the meaning and purpose of life.
The whole aim and end of existence.

Aristotle
Circa 355 BC

Epilogue

THE STRUCTURE and flow of this book is designed to develop a relationship with thought tools and the interlocking matrix by which they are expressed. Some tools will resonate more than others, but do not get stuck on concepts we judge as too simplistic or too complex. The use and integration of one tool can become a miracle that gives freedom from an obstacle that blocks the light of love and joy. Some materials are repeated in many chapters as a reminder that all the material is essential to the whole.

It is my hope that the Spiritual Vision Series and its technology will serve as a lovely rhythm by which recurring themes can be integrated into practical expression in our daily lives. Our commitment to learn consciously through willingness and desire leads to the intake of wisdom. Experience integrates everything into transformative thoughts—and the courage and vigilance to use them frequently.

The spiritual path works best when we are sincere in our attempts to study and practice daily. Once we are aware that we will run into strong resistance and return to old body-mind coping skills, we can use the gift of forgiveness to keep moving forward—despite feelings of failure and disappointment.

The greatest gift we can give ourselves is to stop self-judgment altogether and focus on the usefulness of our choices through awareness. The lack of self-judgment will allow the neutral witness to bring more clarity and remove obstacles, which will allow the flow of joy to be an ever-present partner on the journey (despite external circumstances). We are loved beyond our wildest dreams!

> In the light of clarity, I see you're smiling face,
> In the dark emptiness, I feel your loving embrace.

Rev Dan Costello